Creative
with Cream

Creative with Cream

Over 100 delicious dishes
for every occasion

LORNA WALKER

Octopus Books

First published 1983 by
Octopus Books Limited
59 Grosvenor Street
London W1

This Edition first published 1984
© Octopus Books Limited 1983
ISBN 0 7064 2101 9
Printed in Spain
by Artes Gráficas Toledo, S.A.
D.L.: TO. 53-1984

The photograph on the jacket
shows a cream slice made from
layers of puff pastry sandwiched
with fresh strawberries, strawberry
jam and whipped fresh
double cream.

Contents

Introduction

Whenever friends ask me if I have a recipe for 'something special' I have noticed that the question is asked because they are having visitors, a birthday to celebrate, an anniversary or a special occasion coming up soon. This book has, therefore, been written with my friends in mind and, indeed, all of you who find yourselves cooking for occasions. Instead of dividing the recipes into sections of starters, main dishes and puddings, I've tried to group them roughly into menus for the kind of cooking situation we all find ourselves in from time to time.

There is a lot of controversy over what we consume generally, these days. The important point to remember is that an excess of anything is bad for us and that it is a balanced diet that keeps us healthy. On the same theme, fresh cream should not, strictly speaking, be used as I have done, in every dish in any one menu. Nonetheless, if just one of these recipes should inspire you and suits your situation I hope it will help towards your own more balanced selection. All the recipes can, and should, be used for lots of other occasions and, with a little bit of multiplication or division, to suit any numbers.

When entertaining, part of making visitors welcome is to take that little bit more care over a dish than for every day family fare. However with all the other things there are to do in the home as part of the preparation, and with the lives most of us seem to lead today, who wants to, or has time to, spend hours in the kitchen? With this in mind, the majority of the dishes in this book are quick and simple to prepare – but taste delicious and look impressive. A point worth mentioning here is that although I hope and believe you will find all the dishes delicious, taste is a subjective matter and hence very personal. It is important to taste each dish as you are preparing it so you can adapt flavour and seasoning to your own personal preference. Also, it does not matter whether you use imperial or metric measurements but do stick to only one or the other for best results.

Some people think that if they are entertaining they will be bound to spend a lot of money but, of course, good cooking does not need to be expensive. One of the big pluses of fresh cream is that just a very little stirred into, or topped onto, a dish can make it look extra special. Most of these recipes only use a relatively modest amount of cream, just sufficient to improve the flavour, texture and quality of the dish. However, where I seem to have been blatantly extravagant the number of portions the dish will serve is larger than usual.

In putting my ideas together for this book I would like to thank all those at the Milk Marketing Board for their invaluable help and friendship. Last – but certainly not least – a special thank you to my family for again putting up with a kitchenbound mum and for all their invaluable comments at the 'proof of the pudding' stage of the book.

Fresh Cream – how to choose it and use it

When you order fresh cream from your dairyman, or visit your local grocer or supermarket, there may seem to be a bewildering array of fresh creams available. Here are a few hints to help you find the fresh cream that will suit your needs best.

Double cream is probably the most versatile of all fresh creams as it can be poured, whipped and piped, it floats on soups and coffee and is best for cooking. Its legal minimum butterfat content of 48% makes it easy to whip and even better volume can be obtained by adding a tablespoon of milk to every 150 ml (5 fl oz) double cream.

Whipping cream, with its green cap, is ideal for piping and, despite its lower fat content (of not less than 35%), it will whip to double its volume. An excellent way of making cream go further! Buy it whipped or unwhipped and use to pipe on to cakes and desserts.

Single Cream Add an extra something by pouring single cream over fruit salad or into coffee. This is a cream with a fat content of only 18% (minimum legal limit). Remember, however, that it will not whip or freeze.

Half cream has the lowest minimum fat content, 12%. Again this cannot be whipped but you can serve it poured over your favourite pud to give an extra creamy finish.

Soured cream is ideal for use in savoury dishes or with salad to enhance the flavour and add a refreshing creaminess. This is fresh cream that has been cultured specially to give its distinctive flavour.

Clotted cream is the golden cream traditional to Devon and Cornwall, but now available nationwide. With its distinctive 'nutty' flavour, it is perfect for use with scones and strawberry jam, and it lasts several days in the refrigerator. Try spooning it over apple pie!

Extra thick cream is a wonderful spooning cream. Even though it will not whip it will stay on top of soups and fruit to give that rich luxurious finish.

Frozen cream, which is commercially frozen, is readily available and convenient to keep in the home freezer. For ease of use, frozen cream can be purchased in portions but once thawed it must be used as fresh cream.

Sterilised cream For that unexpected emergency, this is a useful standby for, until it is opened, sterilised cream does not need storing in the refrigerator.

Once you have chosen the fresh cream to suit your needs, remember that it is an easily perishable food that needs to be looked after carefully. Keep it in the refrigerator as much as possible and always follow the '3 Cs' rule – keep it Cool, Clean and Covered. This simple procedure will help to maintain fresh cream's unique flavour and texture which will transform any dish into a treat.

Many recipes require fresh cream to be whipped so that it can be piped or used in mousses or soufflés. To whip fresh cream successfully it must be kept as cool as possible. Remember that it is only possible to whip double and whipping cream.

Freezing cream in general is not necessary as fresh cream is available throughout the year and keeps well for several days in the refrigerator. If you do wish to freeze cream, remember that double cream and whipping cream are the only creams that will freeze successfully. For best results partially whip the cream, place into 300 ml/½ pint cartons leaving space at the top for expansion. Cover with freezer film and seal with tape.

To use the frozen cream, place it in the refrigerator until thawed and then whip the cream carefully to the required thickness.

To whip and pipe cream

1 Start with well chilled bowl and whisk (balloon or spiral) and cold fresh cream. Whip quickly until a matt finish is reached.
Continue more slowly and carefully until the cream stands in peaks on top of the whisk. If cream is over-whipped, butter will be formed.

2 To pipe whipped cream simply and successfully, use a large piping bag, 25-30 cm/10-12 inches long, and a large star nozzle. Place the bag over a grater or tall glass to hold it in place while filling the bag with the whipped cream. This helps to prevent you getting covered as well as the cake!

3 Remove the bag from the grater and gently force the cream into the end of the bag. Twist the bag from the top.
4 Hold the piping bag at the end above the cream – as hot hands will spoil the texture of the cream – and you are ready to pipe stars,

whirls or rosettes on to the cake. Try practising a little at first by piping on to a clean board. Any extra cream can be piped on to a baking tray and frozen, then put into a bag. This is a handy standby for decorating a trifle or sponge.

7

Good Impressions

You want to produce a meal that shows you at your best? Perhaps a new boss or a new mother-in-law to impress? Here are some recipes to suit summer or winter entertaining that should just fit the bill.

SUMMER MENU

CRÈME TAJ MAHAL

An exotic soup to serve on a hot day; mildly curried but with the hint of a sweet-sour flavour.

25 g/1 oz English butter
1 level tablespoon mild curry powder
225 g/8 oz dessert apples, peeled and
   chopped
125 g/4 oz onion, chopped
25 g/1 oz flour
227-g/8-oz can tomatoes
850 ml/1½ pints water
1½ chicken stock cubes
3 tablespoons lemon juice
salt and pepper
65 ml/2½ fl oz fresh single cream

1 Melt the butter in a saucepan, add the curry powder, apple and onion. Gently cook until the onion is soft but not coloured.
2 Blend in the flour and cook for 1 minute.
3 Stir in the canned tomatoes with their juice, the water and the stock cubes. Simmer for 10 minutes then add the lemon juice.
4 Cool the soup, liquidise or press through a sieve, then stir in salt and pepper and half the cream.
5 Chill the soup until required then swirl in the remaining cream and serve.
Note: This soup can also be served hot.
Serves 4-6

TROUT PARCELLED IN SPINACH WITH QUICK SAUCE MOUSSELINE

8 large fresh spinach, sorrel or lettuce leaves
chives, chopped
25 g/1 oz English butter
4 slices lemon
4 cleaned trout
150 ml/¼ pint white wine or dry cider
150 ml/¼ pint water
salt and pepper
lemon slices to garnish

1 Preheat the oven to 160°C/325°F/Gas 3, centre shelf.
2 Plunge the spinach, sorrel or lettuce leaves into a pan of boiling salted water. Remove almost immediately, and rinse in cold water. They should be pliable.
3 Place some chives, a knob of butter and a slice of lemon in the cavity of each trout then firmly wrap each fish in a couple of the blanched leaves.
4 Lay the trout in a shallow buttered dish and pour over the wine or cider and the water. Season with salt and pepper, then cover with foil.
5 Bake the trout for about 20 minutes until tender then lift them on to a hot serving dish. Garnish the fish with lemon slices and serve with baby new potatoes, when in season, and Quick Sauce Mousseline, prepared while the fish is cooking.
Note: The fish can be baked by the same method but without being wrapped in leaves. Both fish and sauce can be served hot or cold.
Serves 4

QUICK SAUCE MOUSSELINE

65 g/2½ oz English butter
2 egg yolks
2 tablespoons lemon juice
150 ml/5 fl oz fresh double cream
salt and pepper to taste

Combine all the ingredients in a bowl over a
saucepan of simmering water. Stir the sauce
continuously over a *low* heat until the mixture
thickens and is hot but not boiling. Remove
from the heat and serve.

HAZELNUT TORTE WITH RASPBERRIES

50 g/2 oz shelled hazelnuts
15 g/½ oz flaked almonds
2 egg whites
125 g/4 oz caster sugar
¼ teaspoon vinegar
¼ teaspoon vanilla essence
225 ml/8 fl oz fresh double cream
3 tablespoons milk
675 g/1½ lb raspberries
2 level tablespoons icing sugar, sifted
25 g/1 oz plain dessert chocolate

1 Preheat the oven to 240°C/475°F/Gas 9, top shelf. Place the hazelnuts in a single layer on a piece of foil and cook for about 5 minutes or grill under a medium heat, turning the nuts frequently, until the skins are dry and the nuts begin to colour. Rub these toasted nuts in a teatowel to flake off their skins. Grind the hazelnuts in a liquidiser or food processor. Toast the almonds under the grill until lightly browned.

2 Reduce the oven temperature to 190°C/375°F/Gas 5, above centre shelf. Grease and line a 20 cm/8 inch sandwich tin with non-stick kitchen paper.

3 Whisk the egg whites until *very* stiff then, while whisking, add the caster sugar, about a level tablespoon at a time. Beat well after each addition. When all the sugar has been added, whisk in the vinegar and vanilla essence. Then fold in the browned hazelnuts until evenly blended.

4 Spread the hazelnut meringue in the prepared tin and smooth level. Bake for about 40 minutes until the crust is firm to a light touch, but the centre remains very slightly soft. Remove from tin and cool.

5 Whip the cream with the milk until softly stiff. Chill.

6 Press 125 g/4 oz of raspberries through a sieve to make a purée then stir in the icing sugar to make a Melba sauce.

7 Before serving, break the chocolate in pieces, place it in the corner of a plastic bag and tie the bag firmly with string just above the chocolate to hold it in the corner of the bag. Place the bag in a pan of hot water to melt the chocolate.

8 Place the meringue cake on a serving dish, spread thickly with the cream then pile the remaining raspberries on top. Dry the plastic bag containing the melted chocolate, cut off a very small hole and squeeze the chocolate to drizzle it over the raspberries. Scatter with the toasted almonds.

9 Cut the torte in wedges to serve and put a little Melba sauce over each portion.
Serves 4-6

WINTER MENU

ARTICHOKE AND TOMATO SOUP WITH CHEESE SOUFFLÉ TOPPING

25 g/1 oz English butter
125 g/4 oz onion, chopped
225 g/8 oz Jerusalem artichokes peeled and chopped
227-g/8-oz can tomatoes
1 clove garlic, crushed (optional)
275 ml/½ pint stock, or water and 1 stock cube
65 ml/2½ fl oz fresh single cream
salt and pepper

Soufflé Topping
15 g/½ oz English butter
1 level tablespoon flour
5 tablespoons milk
25 g/1 oz English Cheddar cheese, grated 1 egg, separated
salt and pepper

1 Melt the butter in a large saucepan and gently fry the onion until soft but not coloured.

2 Add the artichokes to the saucepan and continue cooking slowly for a further 15 minutes.

3 Stir in the canned tomatoes with their juices, the garlic and the stock, then slowly bring to the boil and simmer the vegetables gently for 20-30 minutes until tender.

4 Sieve or liquidise the soup to make a purée then return it to the saucepan.

5 Bring the soup slowly to the boil and simmer for about 5 minutes. Thin down with a little more stock if necessary then remove pan from heat, cool slightly and stir in the cream. Season to taste with salt and pepper.

6 To make the soufflé topping: combine the butter, flour and milk for the topping in a *small* saucepan. Stir continuously over a medium heat until the sauce is thick and smooth. Remove the pan from the heat, add the cheese and stir until it has melted. Stir in the egg yolk, salt and pepper to taste.

7 Preheat the oven to 190°C/375°F/Gas 5, shelf above centre.

8 Divide the soup between 4 small-topped individual ovenproof soup pots then stand them in a baking dish containing hot water about 2.5 cm/1 inch deep.

9 Whisk the egg white until *very* stiff then fold it gently and evenly into the cheese sauce. Divide the mixture between the soup pots.

10 Cook the soup for about 25-30 minutes until the soufflé topping is well puffed up and golden.
Serves 4

Note: This soup is shown in the picture on pages 12 and 13. Providing you have the right shaped, ovenproof soup pots it will be a real winner. However the soup without the topping is delicious in its own right but the ingredients will need to be doubled to serve 4 portions in conventional soup bowls. See also, Note on page 27. When artichokes are out of season, you can use potatoes instead.

OLD ENGLISH STEAK PACKETS WITH SOURED CREAM AND HORSERADISH SAUCE

Although the fillet steaks are small in this recipe – and therefore relatively inexpensive – they are puffed up with mushroom stuffing and pastry to give very healthy-looking portions!

450 g/1 lb fillet steak, in one long piece
50 g/2 oz English butter
125 g/4 oz mushrooms, thinly sliced
25 g/1 oz onion, finely chopped
50 g/2 oz ham, shredded
salt and pepper
crushed garlic
215-g/7½-oz packet frozen puff pastry, thawed
beaten egg to brush
watercress to garnish

1 Trim away any excess fat from the steak and press into a neat shape, then tie it firmly at equal intervals in 4 places to form a roll.
2 Slice the steak through, between each piece of string, to make 4 equal sized steaks.
3 Heat half the butter in a frying pan and when very hot add the steaks; turn them almost immediately so that each side is lightly seared to seal in the juices. Place aside until cold.
4 Add the remaining butter to the pan and lightly fry the mushrooms and onion until the onion is just soft. Add the ham. Turn the mixture together and season well to taste with salt, pepper and lots of crushed garlic. Cool.
5 Roll the pastry out on a lightly floured surface to a rectangle, about 36 x 26 cm/14 x 10 inches, and cut into 4 equal rectangles, roughly 18 x 13 cm/7 x 5 inches.
6 Cut the string away from the steaks. Place a spoonful of the mushroom and ham mixture on each piece of pastry and a steak on top.
7 Brush round the pastry edges with beaten egg then seal over to parcel the steaks.
8 Place the steaks on a baking sheet with sealed edges down. Cover with cling film and chill until ready to cook.
9 Preheat the oven to 230°C/450°F/Gas 8, shelf just above centre.
10 Brush the steak 'packets' with beaten egg then score the pastry by lightly slashing the top of each twice with a sharp knife. Bake the packets in the oven for 15 minutes.
11 When they are cooked, transfer the steaks to a hot serving dish, garnish with watercress and serve immediately with Soured Cream and Horseradish Sauce.
Serves 4

Note: Providing the piece of steak cuts into 4 thick steaks (and not large thin ones) they will be cooked medium/rare.

SOURED CREAM AND HORSERADISH SAUCE

1 tablespoon bottled horseradish sauce or to taste
150 ml/5 fl oz soured cream
salt and pepper

Stir the horseradish sauce into the soured cream. Season with salt and pepper.

ICED MIDNIGHT MINT CREAM

150 ml/5 fl oz fresh single cream
150 ml/5 fl oz fresh double cream
25 g/1 oz icing sugar, sifted
4 to 5 drops green food colouring
½ teaspoon peppermint essence
2 egg whites
50 g/2 oz plain dessert chocolate, finely
    chopped
350-400 g/12-14 oz plain chocolate cake
    covering
additional whipped cream and chocolate
    mint creams (optional)

1 Lightly brush a 1.1 litre/2 pint cake or loaf
tin with oil.
2 Whip the creams together with the icing
sugar, colouring and peppermint essence
until softly stiff. Chill.
3 Whisk the egg whites until very thick and
meringue-like.
4 Fold the whisked whites and chopped
chocolate evenly into the cream then turn
into the prepared tin. Smooth the top level
then freeze until firmly set.
5 Break the chocolate cake covering into

pieces onto a plate, place it over a pan of
gently simmering water until melted.
6 Unmould the iced cream. If the surface is
melting slightly, freeze again until hard then
quickly spread with a very thin layer of the
melted chocolate. Do not worry if the iced
cream is not completely coated. Freeze until
firm.
7 Spread the iced cream with the remaining
chocolate to coat completely. Freeze until
firm then, if liked, decorate the top with
whipped cream and chocolate mint creams.
Leave the iced cream at room temperature
for about 10 minutes before cutting with a
very hot knife.
Serves 8

Note: Chocolate mint creams, melted
gently in a bowl over a pan of simmering
water, can be used to make a softer coating
for the iced cream.

A Family Affair
(catering for 12)

If you are planning a small party to celebrate a wedding or special wedding anniversary, the food helps to create a lasting memory of a special day. The following recipes should do just that.

PHARAOH'S FISH WITH SWEDISH ALMOND SAUCE

As part of a selection of dishes, this recipe made with a 1.5 kg/3 lb fish will serve 10-12 portions. If, however, it is to be the main dish the recipe will need to be doubled for the same number of portions.

1-1.5 kg/2-3 lb large trout, cleaned
50 g/2 oz English butter
6 tablespoons white wine or dry cider
6 tablespoons lemon juice
salt and pepper
75 g/3 oz fresh white breadcrumbs
2 tablespoons fresh double cream, whipped
2 rounded tablespoons thick mayonnaise
lettuce leaves
½ cucumber
sprig of parsley
lemon and gherkin slices to garnish

1 Preheat the oven to 160°C/325°F/Gas 3, centre shelf.
2 Place the fish on a large piece of buttered foil. Spoon the wine or cider and 3 tablespoons of lemon juice over it, then dab with butter and sprinkle with salt and pepper. Wrap the foil over the fish to form a loose parcel and bake for about 45 minutes or until the fish is cooked (the eyes will be white). Cool the fish in the parcel and reserve the liquor.
3 Carefully cut off and reserve both the head and tail of the fish. Remove all skin and bones then flake the flesh into a bowl.
4 Stir 6 tablespoons of the fish liquor into the bowl, add the breadcrumbs, remaining lemon juice, the whipped cream and mayonnaise. Mix well together then season very well to taste with salt and pepper.
5 Spread some lettuce leaves on a large plate. Place the fish head and tail, well apart, on the plate then mound the fish mixture in an oval in between so the fish is restored more or less to its original shape.
6 Cut the cucumber into *wafer-thin* slices and arrange these, like scales, over the fish. Remove fish eyes, or cover with a sprig of parsley. Garnish down the centre of the fish with overlapping lemon slices and then sliced gherkin splayed out fanwise. Serve the fish with Swedish Almond Sauce.
Serves 6-8

SWEDISH ALMOND SAUCE

1 clove garlic, crushed (optional)
25 g/1 oz ground almonds
1 tablespoon finely chopped fresh parsley
    or chives
4 rounded tablespoons thick mayonnaise
125 ml/4 fl oz fresh double cream, whipped
salt and pepper

Stir the garlic, ground almonds, parsley (or chives), mayonnaise and whipped cream together. Season well to taste with salt and pepper.

HAM AND EGG MOUSSE WITH SPICED MAYONNAISE

4 eggs
25 g/1 oz (2 envelopes) gelatine
9 tablespoons cold water
2 chicken stock cubes
50 g/2 oz English butter
50 g/2 oz flour
575 ml/1 pint milk
thinly sliced cucumber
50 g/2 oz ham, sliced
450 g/1 lb ham pieces
275 ml/10 fl oz fresh double cream
salt and pepper

1 Boil the eggs for 10 minutes then drain and cool them in cold water.

2 Stir the gelatine in a measuring jug with 4 tablespoons cold water; leave aside for about 1 minute until it swells. Stir boiling water onto the gelatine to make it up to 275 ml/ ½ pint. Stir in the stock cubes until dissolved.

3 Lightly oil a soufflé dish about 23 cm/ 9 inches in diameter (or use a 2 litre/3½ pint dish). Pour in 4 tablespoons of the gelatine mixture and stir in a further 5 tablespoons cold water. Refrigerate the dish until the gelatine is firmly set.

4 Meanwhile melt the butter in a saucepan, remove from the heat to stir in the flour then smoothly blend in the milk. Stir the sauce over a medium heat until it comes to the boil and is thick and smooth. Stir in the remaining gelatine mixture.

5 Cut the cucumber slices in half and arrange them around the edge of the dish on the set gelatine mixture. Cut the sliced ham into thin strips and arrange these in a trellis pattern in the centre of the dish.

6 Mince all the ham pieces. Peel and chop the eggs. Whip the cream until softly stiff. Stir the ham and eggs into the sauce then blend in the cream. Season to taste.

7 Spoon the ham and egg mousse mixture into the dish. Cover with cling film and refrigerate until firmly set.

8 Dip the dish containing the mousse into hot water for a few seconds. Run a knife around the edge of the dish, cover with a serving plate then turn dish over. The mousse should just slip out; if it doesn't, shake the dish vigorously from *side to side*. Serve the mousse with the Spiced Mayonnaise.
Serves 12-14

SPICED MAYONNAISE

225 g/8 oz tomatoes
3 level tablespoons tomato ketchup
½ level teaspoon paprika
8 rounded tablespoons mayonnaise
Tabasco sauce
salt and pepper

1 Dip the tomatoes in boiling water for a few seconds then remove, cool and peel off skins. Coarsely chop the tomatoes.

2 Combine the tomato ketchup in a bowl with the paprika, mayonnaise and a dash of Tabasco sauce. Stir in the chopped tomatoes then season to taste with salt and pepper.

COLD BEEF STROGANOFF

Although this dish uses an expensive cut of meat, a little of it does go a very long way. If, however, you are working to a budget, a good quality, lean cut of chuck steak works well but you do have to extend the frying time to 15-20 minutes.

675 g/1½ lb lean beef (fillet or sirloin)
flour to coat
salt and pepper
125 g/4 oz English butter
225 g/8 oz button mushrooms, sliced
225 g/8 oz onion, chopped
2 tablespoons lemon juice
275 ml/½ pint canned tomato juice
1 level teaspoon dry mustard
150 ml/5 fl oz fresh double cream, whipped
275 ml/10 fl oz soured cream
chopped chives
sliced tomato, olives and watercress to
  garnish

1 Cut the beef into matchstick strips. Toss them in flour seasoned with salt and pepper.
2 Melt half the butter in a large frying pan and fry the beef over a fairly high heat for about 5 minutes until browned on all sides and cooked. Turn the meat into a bowl.
3 Add the remaining butter to the pan and fry the mushrooms, turning them quickly over a fairly high heat, until cooked. Transfer to the bowl.
4 Add the onion to the pan and fry fairly slowly until soft. Then add to the bowl.
5 Stir the lemon juice, tomato juice and mustard into the meat mixture. Cover and refrigerate until well chilled.
6 Stir the whipped cream into the bowl then half the soured cream. Season to taste with salt and pepper.
7 Serve the stroganoff on a bed of Rice, Celery and Apple Salad. Spoon the

remaining soured cream on top and scatter with chopped chives. Garnish with sliced tomato, olives and watercress.
Serves 10-12

RICE, CELERY AND APPLE SALAD

2 chicken stock cubes
½ level teaspoon turmeric
350 g/12 oz long grain rice
150 ml/¼ pint French dressing
6 sticks celery, thinly sliced
2 dessert apples, cored and thinly sliced
4 tomatoes
salt and pepper

1 Bring 1 litre/1¾ pints water to the boil, stir in the stock cubes and turmeric. When dissolved, add the rice. When the liquid comes to boil again, partially cover the pan and simmer for about 12 minutes until the rice is just tender and most of the stock has been absorbed. Drain well.
2 Pour the French dressing into a bowl, add the drained rice, stir well and leave aside until completely cold.

3 Add the celery and apple to the rice.
4 Dip the tomatoes in boiling water for a few seconds then peel off skins. Chop the tomatoes and add to the rice.
5 Toss the salad well so all ingredients are coated with the dressing. Season well with salt and pepper then toss again.
Serves 12

EASY POTATO SALAD

Hardly a recipe – but so easy it's worth mentioning because it is a useful dish to put out with cold meats when crowd catering.

cold boiled potatoes
very finely chopped onion
thick mayonnaise
soured cream
paprika

Simply cut the potatoes into chunks and spread them out in a fairly thin layer on a shallow dish or plate. Scatter quite thickly with the chopped onion. Combine equal quantities of thick mayonnaise and soured cream then spoon this sauce over the potato to coat. Dust thickly with paprika.

CROQUEMBOUCHE

In France this dish is often served in the way we would serve wedding cake.

Profiteroles
150 g/5 oz English butter
425 ml/¾ pint water
225 g/8 oz plain flour
½ level teaspoon salt
4 eggs
sifted icing sugar to dust
Cream Filling
425 ml/15 fl oz fresh double cream
3 level tablespoons icing sugar, sifted
Caramel
175 g/6 oz caster sugar

1 Preheat the oven to 190°C/375°F/Gas 5, centre and above centre shelves.
2 Gently heat the butter and water together until the butter has melted, then bring to the boil.
3 Meanwhile sift the flour with the salt. Add it all at once as soon as the butter liquid comes to the boil. Beat with a wooden spoon until the mixture is smooth and leaves the sides of the pan. Cool.
4 Whisk the eggs lightly together then beat little by little into the flour mixture, beating well after each addition to give a smoothly blended shiny paste.
5 Either use a teaspoon to place small mounds of the mixture on greased baking sheets or spoon the mixture into a piping bag fitted with a 1 cm/½ inch tube and pipe out small balls about 2.5 cm/1 inch in diameter. Allow room for the mixture to expand during cooking.
6 Place the choux balls in the oven, increasing the heat to 200°C/400°F/Gas 6, and bake for 15 to 20 minutes until puffed up and golden. Cool on a wire rack.
7 To make the filling: whip the cream with the icing sugar until stiff then spoon into a piping bag fitted with a small tube. Press this into the side of each profiterole to fill with cream; alternatively, slit them almost in half and fill with cream.
8 To make the caramel: *gently* heat the caster sugar in a small *heavy* pan, watching and stirring from time to time, until it is pale golden brown.
9 Arrange some of the profiteroles on a large round gold or silver cake board to form a circular shape. Dip the bases of some profiteroles in the hot caramel and arrange in a smaller ring on the original round. Repeat in ever decreasing circles to build up a circular pyramid of profiteroles. Trickle any remaining caramel all over the pyramid. Dust with icing sugar when cold and serve with Chocolate Sauce.
Serves 12

Note: If liked candles may be pressed in, or stuck with caramel, all over the Croquembouche so you carry in a glowing mountain.
Not nearly as difficult as it sounds. Try a dummy run of the profiterole mountain *before* making the caramel so you have worked out the right proportions before starting on the sticking process.
The profiteroles may be made in advance and frozen or stored, unfilled, in a polythene bag. Crisp them up in a hot oven before filling.

CHOCOLATE SAUCE

175 g/6 oz plain dessert chocolate
275 ml/½ pint water
125 g/4 oz sugar

Break the chocolate into a small heavy saucepan. Heat very gently with 3 tablespoons of the water. When the chocolate has melted, stir in the remaining water and the sugar. Continue to heat gently, stirring from time to time until the sugar dissolves, then simmer for about 10 minutes until the sauce is syrupy.

PROFITEROLES WITH CHOCOLATE SAUCE

Make and fill the profiteroles as described then pile them in a serving bowl or basket and serve the Chocolate Sauce separately. (An easier alternative!)

MERINGUE SWANS WITH MELBA SAUCE

These swans make a spectacular dessert if, for fun, you serve them on a small mirror or stainless steel platter decorated with some fresh flowers so they look as if they are sailing on a lake with waterlilies.

4 egg whites (size 1, 2)
225 g/8 oz caster sugar
675 g/1½ lb raspberries
75 g/3 oz icing sugar, sifted
450 ml/15 fl oz fresh double cream

1 Preheat the oven to 140°C/275°F/Gas 1, lowest shelves.
2 Line 3 or 4 baking sheets with non-stick kitchen paper.
3 Whisk the egg whites together until *very* stiff.
4 Then, while whisking, add the sugar, about a level tablespoon at a time, whisking very well after each addition. When all the sugar has been added, the mixture should be marshmallowy in texture.
5 Spoon the mixture into a piping bag fitted with a 1.5cm/½ inch plain tube. Pipe 12 elongated ovals about 8 cm/3 inches long onto a baking sheet. These are the bases.

6 Now pipe 12 reversed 'S' shapes, each about 8 cm/3 inches long, to make the combined heads and necks. Finally pipe 12 figure '6' and then 12 reversed '6' each about 6 cm/2¾ inches long to make the wings.
7 Cook the meringues for 1½ to 2 hours until crisp, changing the tins around so they cook evenly to a very pale gold colour.
8 Press 350 g/12 oz of the raspberries through a nylon sieve to make a purée then stir in the icing sugar to make the Melba sauce.
9 Whip the cream until stiff, then pipe or pile it on the swan bases. Lightly press the neck meringues at one end and the wings on either side. Pile the remaining raspberries between the swans' wings. Serve the Melba sauce separately.
Makes 12

Note: Check the oven shelf arrangements before starting this recipe as it may be necessary to prepare the swans in two batches in order to accommodate them all in the oven. If you've never tried piping before, now is the time to give it a whirl. If you just can't get the knack, the swans can easily be re-shaped with a spoon to make Pavlovas (see page 78)!

STRAWBERRY CREAM TORTE

15 g/½ oz (1 envelope) gelatine
juice of ½ lemon
4 tablespoons water
275 ml/10 fl oz fresh double cream
75 g/3 oz icing sugar, sifted
275 ml/½ pint unsweetened strawberry purée
   (made from 350 g/12 oz strawberries)
4 eggs, separated
125 g/4 oz caster sugar
125 g/4 oz plain flour
salt
7 whole strawberries to decorate

1 Preheat the oven to 190°C/375°F/Gas 5, centre shelf. Grease two 20-23 cm/8-9 inch sandwich tins or a 23 cm/9 inch springform cake tin and line the bases with greased greaseproof paper.
2 Place the gelatine in a small bowl, stir in the lemon juice and the water. Leave aside for the gelatine to swell. Place the bowl over a saucepan of hot water; heat until the gelatine has dissolved.
3 Whip the cream with the icing sugar until stiff.
4 Stir the dissolved gelatine into the strawberry purée and make it up to 575 ml/1 pint with cold water if necessary.
5 Combine the strawberry purée mixture with the cream. Stir, cover and refrigerate until setting. (This can take up to 3 hours.)
6 To make the sponge cake: whisk the egg whites until very stiff and meringue-like. In another bowl whisk the egg yolks and caster sugar together until thick, foamy and much paler in colour. Combine the whisked egg yolks with the whites and continue whisking until the mixture is evenly blended and still thick and foamy.
7 Gently fold the sieved flour and salt into the egg mixture until evenly mixed. Divide between the sandwich tins or spread into the springform tin.
8 Bake the cake for about 20 minutes for the 2 tins or 40 minutes for the single tin. They should be firm to a light touch. Turn out on to a wire rack and leave to cool.
9 Cut the cake into 4 layers. Use about half the strawberry cream to sandwich the layers of cake together and use the remainder to cover the cake completely, smoothing it off finally with a hot palette knife. Carefully lift it on to a serving plate then decorate with whole strawberries. Chill in the refrigerator until firmly set. Serve as a cake or as a dessert.
Serves 12

Note: When strawberries are out of season, any other fruit purée can be used instead.

Just the Two of Us

Shop for these easy-to-buy ingredients, perhaps on the way home from work, for a spur of the moment invitation. Alternatively make these simple dishes in advance for that special occasion when two is company whether young or old.

GREEN PEA AND MINT SOUP

15 g/½ oz English butter
125 g/4 oz frozen peas
25 g/1 oz onion, finely chopped
2 level teaspoons cornflour
275 ml/½ pint milk
1 chicken stock cube
¼-½ teaspoon finely chopped fresh mint or
   ¼ teaspoon dried
salt and pepper
3 tablespoons fresh single cream
sprig of mint or parsley to garnish (optional)

1 Gently melt the butter in a saucepan, add the frozen peas and onion. Cook *very* slowly in the covered pan, stirring frequently, until the peas are soft and pulpy.
2 Liquidise or sieve the cooked peas and onion with 150 ml/¼ pint water, to make a purée.
3 Smoothly blend the cornflour with the milk, add to the puréed peas with the stock cube and mint.
4 Bring the soup slowly to the boil, stirring. Season to taste with salt and pepper. Cool the soup slightly before stirring in the cream. Serve with a sprig of mint or parsley to garnish, if liked.
Serves 2

CHICKEN TENERIFE

25 g/1 oz English butter
1 rasher bacon, shredded
15 g/½ oz blanched and flaked almonds
1 small banana
flour to dredge
2 chicken breasts (or other portions)
salt and pepper
paprika
25 g/1 oz onion, chopped
½ level tablespoon flour
1 tablespoon brandy (optional)
6 tablespoons chicken stock
3 tablespoons fresh single cream

1 Melt half the butter in a frying pan and fry the bacon and nuts until lightly browned; remove them to a plate.
2 Slice the banana diagonally and dredge in flour then fry until lightly browned. Remove to the plate.
3 Coat the chicken in flour seasoned with salt, pepper and paprika. Add the remaining butter to the frying pan and fry the chicken for about 5 minutes over a medium heat until it is browned on all sides.
4 Add the chopped onion to the pan, cover and cook very slowly for a further 15-20 minutes until the chicken is cooked. Remove the chicken and keep warm.
5 Blend the ½ level tablespoon flour into the pan then the brandy, if using, and the stock. Stir, bring the sauce to the boil, then remove the pan from the heat to stir in the cream. Cook until the sauce is thickening then add the nuts, bacon and finally the bananas. Season well to taste and pour over the chicken. Dust with paprika.
Serves 2

CREAMED HONEY AND BRANDY POSSET

65 ml/2½ fl oz fresh double cream
½-1 tablespoon clear honey
1 tablespoon brandy
1 egg white
2 hazelnuts
ground cinnamon or nutmeg to dust

1 Whip the cream until softly stiff then trickle in the honey and brandy. Continue whipping until thick; chill.
2 Whisk the egg white until very stiff then fold into the cream mixture.
3 Divide this creamy posset between 2 small individual dishes and serve each topped with a hazelnut and dusted with a little cinnamon or nutmeg.
Note: This dessert can also be frozen and served as an iced cream.
Serves 2

23

Made in Minutes

Quick to make dishes, when you haven't time to spare: but keep that a secret!

SMOKED MACKEREL OR TROUT WITH APPLE AND HORSERADISH SAUCE

130-g/4.59-oz can apple sauce
150 ml/5 fl oz soured cream
1 teaspoon tarragon vinegar
4 level teaspoons horseradish sauce
salt and pepper
6 small portions of smoked mackerel or trout
lettuce, sliced lemon, red-skinned apple and
   paprika to garnish (optional)

1 Turn the apple sauce into a small jug or bowl. Stir in the cream, vinegar and horseradish sauce. Season with salt and pepper to taste.

2 Arrange the fish (about 50 g/2 oz fillet each is the right size, if to be served as a starter) on small plates; garnish with lettuce, lemon and apple slices, if liked. Pour just a little of the sauce over each fillet and dust with paprika. Serve the remaining sauce separately.
Serves 6

SAUTÉED PORK WITH SAGE

450 g/1 lb pork tenderloin or leg fillet
about 65 g/2½ oz English butter
125 g/4 oz onion, sliced
225 g/8 oz mushrooms, sliced
3 level tablespoons flour
275 ml/½ pint stock
2 tablespoons dry white vermouth (optional)
½ level teaspoon dried sage
2 level tablespoons finely chopped capers
150 ml/5 fl oz fresh single cream
salt and pepper

1 Shred the pork into matchstick strips.
2 Heat 25 g/1 oz of the butter in a fairly large frying pan, and fry the pork over a high heat for 5-10 minutes, turning it frequently until becoming golden brown. Remove to a plate with a slotted spoon.

3 Add the sliced onion and fry over a medium heat until soft, adding more butter if necessary. Remove to the plate.

4 Heat the remaining butter in the pan and fry the sliced mushrooms until just soft, then remove them to the plate.

5 Remove the pan from the heat to blend in the flour, stock and vermouth, if using, then add the pork, onion, mushrooms and sage. Stir over a medium heat until the sauce thickens.

6 Add the capers and cream, season to taste with salt and pepper (adding more sage and capers, if liked) then allow the mixture to come almost to the boil and stir until the sauce is thick and creamy.

7 Serve with plain boiled rice or buttered noodles.

Serves 4-6

RUSSIAN CHICKEN

4-6 chicken breasts, boned
50 g/2 oz English butter
125 g/4 oz button mushrooms, sliced
1½ level tablespoons flour
150 ml/¼ pint chicken stock
150 ml/5 fl oz soured cream
2-3 tablespoons vodka
salt and pepper
paprika

1 Fry the chicken breasts in the butter until cooked through and pale golden brown. Transfer to a shallow ovenproof dish and keep them hot.

2 Add the sliced mushrooms to the frying pan and fry until tender and turning golden. Spoon over the chicken.

3 Stir the flour into the pan residue then gradually blend in the chicken stock. Stir over a medium heat to make a thick sauce. Cool slightly then stir in the soured cream.

4 Mix in the vodka and salt and pepper to taste, then pour the sauce over the chicken. Serve dusted with paprika.

Serves 4-6

Note: Good with buttered noodles, baby beets and green beans or a salad. Instead of vodka you can substitute gin.

Filling the Gaps

Friends coming who might stay on
for a light lunch or supper?
Then if you want something a little
bit different one of the following
recipes might fill the bill.

FRIED CHEESE WITH CRUNCHY SALAD

225 g/8 oz English Cheddar cheese
1 egg (size 6), beaten
breadcrumbs, fresh or golden
50 g/2 oz English butter
lemon wedges to garnish

1 Choose a firm Cheddar cheese and cut it into 5 mm/¼ inch thick slices.
2 Brush the cheese with beaten egg and coat in the breadcrumbs.

3 Heat the butter in a frying pan and, when very hot and frothing, fry the cheese quickly on each side for barely ¼ minute so that the crumbs become crisp and the cheese is just starting to melt.
4 Serve the fried cheese immediately, with lemon wedges and Crunchy Salad.
Serves 4

CRUNCHY SALAD

¼ cucumber, diced
125 g/4 oz Chinese leaves, shredded
1 dessert apple, cored and sliced
2 sticks celery, chopped
½ green pepper, deseeded and chopped
2 tablespoons French dressing
4 tomatoes, sliced
65 g/2½ oz natural yogurt
2 tablespoons fresh single cream
1 clove garlic, crushed (optional)
salt and pepper
50 g/2 oz onion, sliced
25 g/1 oz black olives (optional)

Combine the diced cucumber with the shredded Chinese leaves, apple, celery and

green pepper. Toss with the French dressing.
Arrange in a salad bowl and place the sliced
tomatoes on top. Combine the natural
yogurt with the cream, garlic, if using, and salt
and pepper to taste. Spoon this dressing over
the salad just before serving. Top with the
sliced onion and black olives, if using.

POACHED EGGS WITH ARTICHOKE SAUCE

50 g/2 oz onion, finely chopped
75 g/3 oz English butter
225 g/8 oz Jerusalem artichokes, peeled and
    coarsely chopped
275 ml/½ pint stock
4 rounds French bread
4 small eggs (size 6)
65 ml/2½ fl oz fresh single cream
salt and pepper
chopped parsley

1 Place the onion in a saucepan with
25 g/1 oz of the butter over a very gentle heat.
2 Prepare the Jerusalem artichokes and add
to the saucepan.
3 Cook for 5 minutes then add the stock,
cover and simmer for 15 minutes until soft.
Sieve or liquidise the pan contents together.
4 Melt the remaining 50 g/2 oz butter and fry
the rounds of French bread until crisp and
golden on both sides. Keep croûtes hot in a
low oven.
5 Meanwhile poach the eggs until just set.
6 Stir the cream into the artichoke purée
and very gently reheat. Season to taste with
salt and pepper.
7 Arrange the croûtes on individual plates,
top with poached eggs and coat with the
sauce. Serve sprinkled with a little parsley.
Serves 4

Note: You can now buy or grow Jerusalem
artichokes that really have very few knobs. So
peel them just like potatoes, discarding the
knobs as you go. When artichokes are out of
season, the sauce is also good made in the
same way with potatoes, and the addition of
50 g/2 oz grated English Cheddar cheese.

BAKED POTATOES STUFFED WITH MUSHROOMS AND HAM

4 large potatoes
50 g/2 oz English butter
25 g/1 oz onion, very finely chopped
125 g/4 oz mushrooms, very finely chopped
50 g/2 oz cooked ham, minced or finely
    chopped
65 ml/2½ fl oz fresh single cream
salt and pepper
25 g/1 oz English Cheddar cheese, grated
2 rounded tablespoons mayonnaise
1 tablespoon finely chopped chives

1 Preheat the oven to 200°C/400°F/Gas 6,
shelf above centre.
2 Prick the potatoes in several places with a
fork and bake them for about 1 hour until
they feel soft when lightly squeezed.
3 Melt about 25 g/1 oz of the butter and
gently fry the onion and mushrooms until
soft but not coloured.
4 Cut a thin slice off the top of each cooked
potato. Holding them with an oven glove,
scoop the potato flesh into a bowl taking care
not to damage skin. Mash the potato well.
5 Stir the cooked mushroom and onion
into the potato with the ham, about
2 tablespoons of the cream and the remaining
butter. Beat well and season to taste.
6 Spoon the potato mixture back into the
shells and scatter with cheese.
7 When required, reduce the oven
temperature to 190°C/375°F/Gas 5 and reheat
the potatoes for about 20 minutes.
8 Mix the remaining cream with the
mayonnaise and chopped chives. Season to
taste with salt and pepper. Serve this sauce
separately with the stuffed potatoes.
Serves 4

Note: For a change, replace the ham with
50-125 g/2-4 oz peeled prawns and add lemon
juice to taste.

HUNGARIAN BEEF SOUP WITH PICKLED CUCUMBER AND SOURED CREAM

A heartwarming winter soup that is a meal in itself. Canned broad or butter beans may be added and dumplings too, if you want to make it even more substantial. The cucumber and soured cream really make it, so don't be tempted to leave them out.

125 g/4 oz onion, chopped
225 g/8 oz minced beef
25 g/1 oz English butter
350 g/12 oz potatoes, diced
227-g/8-oz can tomatoes
850 ml/1½ pints stock
salt and pepper
2 cloves garlic, crushed
3 or 4 pickled cucumbers, sliced
4 tablespoons soured cream

1 Fry the chopped onion and minced beef in the butter until lightly browned.
2 Add the diced potato and fry for a further 2-3 minutes.
3 Stir in the canned tomatoes with their juice, the stock, salt, pepper and garlic. Simmer gently for 30 minutes, then add the sliced pickled cucumbers.
4 Ladle the soup into bowls and swirl in the soured cream.
Serves 6-8

SEA-CHICKEN PIE

125 g/4 oz green pepper, thinly sliced
125 g/4 oz onion, thinly sliced
65 g/2½ oz English butter
50 g/2 oz flour
275 ml/½ pint milk
1 chicken stock cube
150 ml/5 fl oz fresh single cream
198-g/7-oz can tuna
125 g/4 oz cooked chicken, chopped
1 level tablespoon capers, finely chopped (optional)
salt and pepper
370-g/13-oz packet frozen puff pastry, thawed

1 Slowly fry the pepper and onion in the butter until soft. Remove from the pan with a slotted spoon and place aside.

3 Mix the flour into the butter in the pan then blend in the milk and the stock cube. Slowly bring the sauce to the boil, stirring. Cool slightly then stir in the cream, green pepper, onion, drained tuna, chicken and chopped capers. Season to taste with salt and pepper. Cool.

3 Preheat the oven to 220°C/425°F/Gas 7, shelf above centre.

4 Divide the pastry in 2, one piece a little larger than the other, then roll out the larger piece to line a 23 cm/9 inch loose based flan or sandwich tin.

5 Spread the filling in the lined tin.

6 Roll out the remaining pastry to a neat round to fit the top of the pie. Using a sharp knife mark with a trellis pattern. Place on the pie, seal edges.

7 Brush the top of the pie with a little extra cream and bake for about 40 minutes until the pastry is golden brown and cooked through. Serve the pie hot or cold.

Serves 6-8

THE ABBOT'S FAVOURITE SUPPER

2 ripe fresh pears or 4 canned pear halves
50 g/2 oz Blue Stilton cheese
6 tablespoons fresh single cream
2 rounded tablespoons mayonnaise
1/8 teaspoon dried tarragon
2 level teaspoons tarragon vinegar
1 level tablespoon caster sugar
salt and pepper
4 slices thickly buttered brown bread
4 slices ham
lettuce leaves
paprika

1 Peel, halve and core the fresh pears or place the canned pears on a plate to drain.

2 Mash the cheese with about 2 tablespoons of the cream until it is soft. Stuff this mixture into the pear cavities.

3 Combine the mayonnaise with the tarragon, vinegar, caster sugar and remaining cream. Season to taste with salt and pepper.

4 Arrange the slices of buttered brown bread on 4 plates and top each with a slice of ham, lettuce leaves, and a stuffed pear. Coat the pears with the tarragon mayonnaise and a dusting of paprika.

Serves 4

Outdoor Living

*It's a shame we can't rely enough on
our English weather to entertain
regularly with the so-easy barbecue.
Here's a barbecue menu that,
even if the weather changes,
is worth smoking out the
garage to try!*

INDONESIAN-STYLE BARBECUED PORK WITH PINEAPPLE

Marinade
2 tablespoons soy sauce
2 tablespoons hot water
1 level tablespoon honey
1 level tablespoon brown sugar
¼ teaspoon freshly ground black pepper
2 cloves garlic, crushed
1 tablespoon cooking oil
75 g/3 oz onion, finely chopped
3 level tablespoons tomato ketchup

6 pork chops
1 fresh pineapple or 432-g/15-oz can sliced
　　pineapple
2 level tablespoons peanut butter
1 level teaspoon cornflour
½-1 level teaspoon ground cumin
1-2 level teaspoons desiccated coconut
salt and pepper
1-2 tablespoons fresh double cream

1 Mix all the ingredients for the marinade in
a fairly large bowl, stir well then add the pork
chops (spare rib chops are good) and turn
them in the marinade so they are well coated.
Cover the bowl with cling film and refrigerate
for at least 4 hours but preferably overnight.
2 Cut the fresh pineapple into 6 slices or
drain the canned pineapple slices and
reserve the juice for the sauce.

3 Measure 175 ml/6 fl oz water or make the
pineapple juice up to this amount with water.
4 Mix the peanut butter with the cornflour,
cumin and desiccated coconut and gradually
blend in the water or mixture of water and
pineapple juice.
5 Prepare the barbecue and, when it is very
hot, carefully lift the meat from the marinade,
shaking off the residue, and cook over the hot
embers for about 7 minutes on each side
until it is a rich brown and cooked through.
Grill the pineapple slices.
6 While the meat is cooking, stir the
marinade into the peanut butter mixture
then turn this into a small saucepan and stir
over a medium heat until it comes to the boil
and is slightly thick. Season to taste with salt
and pepper then stir in the 1-2 tablespoons
cream according to taste. It is important to try
the sauce at this stage as it has a fairly full
flavour and the cream has the effect of
blending the flavours together.
7 Serve the grilled meat and pineapple
coated with the sauce. Accompany with plain
boiled rice.
Serves 6
Note: Both the marinade and sauce combine
to make this a tasty barbecue recipe. Having
tried it once you might like to increase the
quantity of spice to taste, even adding a little
chilli powder. You will then need to add a
little more cream.

LEMON, NUT AND THYME DRESSING

This dressing transforms a plain green salad.
Try serving small portions of the salad as a
starter before a summer meal.

150 ml/5 fl oz fresh single cream
2 tablespoons lemon juice
50 g/2 oz mixed nuts, chopped
25 g/1 oz raisins (optional)
salt and pepper
chopped fresh thyme

Combine the cream with the lemon juice,
mixed nuts and raisins, if using. Season to
taste with salt, pepper and thyme.

ANN'S FRUIT CREAM

Besides the fresh summer berries, frozen or canned fruit may be used to make this refreshing dessert at any time of the year.

450 g/1 lb mixed soft red fruit (raspberries, redcurrants, strawberries, etc)
275 ml/½ pint sweet cider
2 level tablespoons cornflour
6-8 level tablespoons caster sugar
150 ml/5 fl oz fresh double cream
2 tablespoons milk

1 Set aside about 12 raspberries or other soft fruit for decoration.
2 Press the remaining fruit through a nylon sieve (or liquidise then sieve to remove pips) to make a purée. Add the cider.
3 Blend the cornflour in a bowl with 2 tablespoons water, stir in the fruit purée and sugar. Pour the mixture into a saucepan and slowly bring to the boil, stirring. Cook for 1 minute, taste, adding more sugar if necessary.
4 Cool the fruit mixture a little then pour it into 4-6 small individual dishes. Cover and chill for at least 3 hours.
5 Whip the cream and milk together until softly stiff then mix in or spread over the chilled fruit mixture and decorate with the reserved soft fruit.
Serves 4-6
Note: To follow this recipe using frozen or canned fruit you will need to make 375 ml/¾ pint fruit purée.

Pick-Your-Own

Make the most of autumn fruit when it's cheap to buy or when your fruit trees surprise you with their abundance.

PEAR AND RATAFIA PIE

225 g/8 oz self-raising flour
¼ teaspoon salt
175 g/6 oz English butter
4-5 tablespoons cold milk
150 g/5 oz granulated sugar
425 ml/¾ pint water
900 g/2 lb pears
50-g/2-oz packet dry ratafias or macaroons
2-3 tablespoons sherry or Marsala
65 ml/2½ fl oz fresh double cream
15 g/½ oz caster sugar
icing sugar to dust (optional)

1 Measure the flour and salt into a bowl, add the butter, cut it in with a knife then rub in until it looks like breadcrumbs. Sprinkle in sufficient milk to bind the mixture together to form a dough.

2 Wrap the dough in cling film and chill.
3 Dissolve the granulated sugar in the water by heating gently. Stir from time to time.
4 Peel, quarter and core the pears, add to the pan and cook until just soft.
5 Remove the pears from the pan with a slotted spoon and leave to cool on a plate.
6 Preheat the oven to 200°C/400°F/Gas 6, shelf above centre.
7 Place the ratafias or macaroons on a plate and spoon the sherry or Marsala over them.
8 Cut the pastry in half and roll each piece out thinly to fit a 23 cm/9 inch pie plate.
9 Take one pastry round, fold it in half and cut 1 cm/⅜ inch slits to within 2.5 cm/1 inch from the edge.
10 Line the pie plate with the uncut pastry round, cover with the cold pears then arrange the soaked ratafias or macaroons on top. Pour over the cream and any remaining wine.
11 Carefully unfold the slit round of pastry on top of the pears, seal the edges together with water then trim and decorate the edge.
12 Brush the top of the pie lightly with cream or water then sprinkle heavily with the caster sugar.
13 Bake the pie for about 40 minutes until the pastry is crisp and cooked. Serve hot or cold dusted with icing sugar, if liked.
Serves 6

FRENCH APRICOT AND APPLE DESSERT

50 g/2 oz granulated sugar
½ stick cinnamon or ¼ teaspoon ground
curl of orange rind
225 g/8 oz apples, dessert or cooking
3-4 croissants
75 g/3 oz demerara sugar
219-g/7¾-oz can apricot halves
2 level teaspoons cornflour
2 tablespoons kirsch or brandy (optional)
150 ml/5 fl oz fresh double cream
¼ teaspoon vanilla essence
1 level teaspoon caster sugar
15 g/½ oz toasted almonds

1   Combine the granulated sugar, cinnamon and orange curl with 150 ml/
¼ pint water in a small saucepan. Stir over a low heat until the sugar has dissolved.
2   Peel and thinly slice the apples, then gently poach them in the sugar syrup for about 5 minutes until they are just tender. Cool and drain, reserving the syrup.
3   Using a very sharp knife, cut the croissants into very thin slices. Arrange these on a grill rack and sprinkle thickly with the demerara sugar. Grill until the sugar is starting to melt and brown lightly. Cool.
4   Arrange the sugared slices in rings on 4-6 small plates.
5   Drain and mix the apricots with the apples, adding the apricot syrup to the reserved apple syrup. Blend the cornflour with 1 tablespoon of the syrup. Measure 150 ml/¼ pint of the syrup into a saucepan (making up with water if necessary) then bring it to the boil and stir into the blended cornflour. Return this sauce to the pan and boil until it is clear and syrupy. Flavour with kirsch or brandy, if liked.
6   Whip the cream until stiff with the vanilla essence and caster sugar.
7   Pile the fruit on the croissant rings, pipe or spoon on peaks of the cream and sprinkle with the toasted nuts. Serve the sauce separately.
Serves 4-6

Note: An easy and effective dessert to make. Instead of individual portions, you can make a larger more decorative dessert by preparing more fruit and croissants then layering it. Start with a fairly large ring of croissants and a layer of fruit and cream and then continue with smaller rings, finishing with a topping of cream and nuts so it is all layered up into a pyramid.

PLUM MOUSSE

50 g/2 oz granulated sugar and 450 g/
   1 lb plums, halved and stoned, or
   564-g/1-lb 4-oz can Victoria plums
2 tablespoons lemon juice
15 g/¼ oz gelatine
½ level teaspoon ground cinnamon
65 ml/2½ fl oz port (optional)
2 egg whites
75 g/3 oz demerara sugar
150 ml/5 fl oz fresh double cream
additional whipped cream to decorate
   (optional)
ground cinnamon for dusting (optional)

1 If using fresh plums dissolve the granulated sugar in 150 ml/¼ pint water. Add the stoned plums and simmer *very* gently for about 15 minutes until tender.
2 Drain the cooked or canned plums, reserving 150 ml/¼ pint of the syrup. Press the plums through a nylon sieve to make 275 ml/½ pint purée.
3 Measure the lemon juice in a cup and stir in the gelatine; leave aside to swell.
4 Gently heat 6 ml/2½ fl oz of the reserved fruit syrup with the cinnamon, remove the pan from the heat, add the gelatine and stir until dissolved. Add the port *or* remaining 65 ml/2½ fl oz reserved fruit syrup. Cool, stir in the plum purée and refrigerate until syrupy.
5 Whisk the egg whites until very stiff, continue whisking adding the demerara sugar a tablespoon at a time, then mix in the purée.
6 Whip the cream and fold into the mousse mixture until evenly blended then divide it between 6-8 individual dishes or pour into a 1.1 litre/2 pint dish. Refrigerate until firmly set then decorate, if liked, with more whipped cream and a dusting of cinnamon.
Serves 6-8

MALABAR APPLES
(Poached apples coated with a ginger cream)

125 g/4 oz granulated sugar
curl of orange rind
curl of lemon rind
½ stick cinnamon
2 cloves
275 ml/½ pint water
4 dessert apples (Cox's are good)
4 ginger biscuits
1 egg white
150 ml/¼ pint fresh double cream
1 teaspoon vanilla essence
1 level tablespoon soft brown sugar
1 level teaspoon ground ginger
8 pieces crystallised ginger, chopped

1   Place the granulated sugar in a saucepan with the orange and lemon rind, cinnamon, cloves and 275 ml/½ pint water. Heat and slowly dissolve the sugar, stirring from time to time.
2   Peel and core the apples, without removing the stalks, then place them in the saucepan. Cover, bring to the boil, then immediately reduce the heat and simmer *gently* for 5 to 10 minutes or until the apples are just tender. Cool them in the syrup then drain.
3   Place ginger biscuits on 4 little plates, sprinkle each with about 1 tablespoon of the sugar syrup.
4   Whisk the egg white until very stiff. Whip the cream with the vanilla essence, brown sugar and ginger. Fold in the egg white.
5   Swirl this cream over the apples to coat. Lift them (by the stalks) on to the serving plates and scatter with chopped crystallised ginger.
Serves 4

Note: Pears poached with apricots are also good served with this ginger cream.

SPICED ORCHARD CHEESECAKE

1½ level teaspoons gelatine
juice of ½ lemon
450 g/1 lb cooking apples
125 g/4 oz English butter
¼ level teaspoon ground mixed spice
¼ level teaspoon ground cinnamon
75 g/3 oz caster sugar
150 g/5 oz fruit and spice or ginger biscuits, crushed
225 g/8 oz full fat soft cheese
25 g/1 oz raisins (optional)
1 egg white
150 ml/¼ pint fresh double cream
2 red-skinned dessert apples to decorate (optional)
lemon juice (optional)

1   Place the gelatine in a cup and stir in the lemon juice. Leave aside for a few minutes to swell.
2   Peel, core and slice the apples then place in a saucepan with 50 g/2 oz of the butter, the mixed spice, cinnamon and caster sugar. Cook very gently until the apples are soft then stir in the gelatine mixture to dissolve. Sieve the apple mixture into a bowl to make a purée.
3   Melt the remaining butter, stir in the crushed biscuits and spread this crumb crust in a 20 cm/8 inch flan tin or dish, patting it evenly over the base and sides.
4   Soften the cheese in a bowl, beat in the cooled apple purée mixture and stir in the raisins, if using.
5   Whisk the egg white until very stiff. Whip the cream until softly stiff. Fold both the whisked white and the cream carefully into the apple mixture until evenly blended, then spread smoothly on top of the crumb crust.
6   Cover the flan dish with cling film and chill until the filling is firmly set. Decorate if liked with the dessert apples, unpeeled but thinly sliced and painted with lemon juice to prevent their turning brown.
Serves 6-8

Cool It!

A menu for a really hot day, equally good with chilled white wine, ice-cold lager, or why not ice-cold milk?

CREAMED GAZPACHO

With the aid of an electric food processor or liquidiser this is a double quick 'flick of the switch' recipe!

1 chicken stock cube
½ cucumber, peeled and roughly chopped
50 g/2 oz onion, roughly chopped
1 green pepper, halved and deseeded
540-ml/19-fl oz can tomato juice
150 ml/5 fl oz fresh single cream
1-2 cloves garlic, crushed
juice of ½ lemon
salt and pepper

1 Dissolve the stock cube in a little boiling water then make it up to 275 ml/½ pint with cold water.
2 Finely mince the cucumber, onion and green peppers (or liquidise with some of the liquid).
3 Stir in all the remaining ingredients and season well to taste with salt and pepper.
4 Chill for at least an hour before serving.
Serves 6-8

SLICED MEAT IN MEDITERRANEAN SAUCE

100-g/3½-oz can tuna fish
3 rounded tablespoons thick mayonnaise
65 ml/2½ fl oz fresh single cream
1 tablespoon lemon juice
salt and pepper
225 g/8 oz *very* thinly sliced cooked pork
sliced lemon
1-2 hard-boiled eggs
2 teaspoons capers
50-g/1¾-oz can anchovy fillets, drained
paprika

1 Liquidise the drained tuna, mayonnaise, cream and lemon juice together (or mash the tuna very finely and mix thoroughly with the remaining ingredients). Season this mayonnaise mixture well to taste with salt and pepper.
2 Arrange the thinly-sliced meat in a single layer on a serving plate. Coat with the mayonnaise sauce.
3 Garnish with sliced lemon, hard-boiled egg, a scattering of capers and slivers of anchovy. Dust with paprika. Good served with a tomato and onion salad, chopped lettuce and cooked potatoes tossed in vinaigrette.
Serves 6
Note: Although pork is used in the recipe, almost any meat is good in this sauce, particularly chicken.

ANNA'S CRÈME CHANTILLY

A friend produced this pudding for lunch on a steamy hot day – it was served well chilled and was heavenly! The nuts are Anna's idea as the original recipe was topped with grated chocolate.

575 ml/1 pint milk
3 eggs
2 level tablespoons caster sugar
½ teaspoon vanilla essence
25 g/1 oz flaked blanched almonds
1½ tablespoons apricot jam
65 ml/2½ fl oz fresh double cream

1 Preheat the oven to 180°C/350°F/Gas 4, centre shelf.
2 Slowly bring the milk almost to boiling point. Remove from the heat.
3 Separate one of the eggs and place the white aside.
4 Whisk the whole eggs plus the yolk in a bowl with the sugar and vanilla essence. Stir in the hot milk.
5 Strain this custard into a 1 litre/1¾ pint ovenproof dish. Stand it in a tin half-filled with hot water. Cover the dish with foil and cook for about 1 hour or until firm to the touch. Leave aside until cold.
6 Meanwhile, spread the blanched almonds

on a piece of foil and bake on the shelf above centre for about 15 minutes or until crisp and golden. Place aside.

7 Spread the apricot jam over the cooled thick custard.

8 Whisk the reserved egg white until very stiff. Whip the cream until stiff and fold both together then spread over the cold custard. Chill.

9 Just before serving, scatter with the almonds.

Serves 6

Iced Wonders

Iced creams with a difference!

ICED CREAM WATERMELON

175 g/6 oz granulated sugar
125 g/4 oz redcurrants or raspberries
red food colouring (optional)
finely grated rind and juice of ½ orange
1 medium-sized green-skinned honeydew
   melon
⅛ level teaspoon ground ginger
about 2 drops green food colouring
1 egg white
275 ml/10 fl oz fresh double cream
raisins or prunes (optional)

1 Stir the granulated sugar with 425 ml/
¾ pint water in a saucepan over a low heat.
When the sugar has dissolved increase the
heat and bring to the boil; boil gently for 10
minutes then place aside to cool.
2 Put the redcurrants (or raspberries) in a
saucepan with 2 tablespoons cold water.

Cook gently for about 10 minutes or until soft
then rub through a nylon sieve to make a
purée. Stir in red colouring as necessary.
3 Measure 200 ml/7 fl oz of the sugar syrup in
a measuring jug. Add the redcurrant or
raspberry purée, orange rind and juice. Make
up to 275 ml/½ pint with cold water if
necessary. Place aside.
4 Cut the melon in half and remove the
seeds then scoop out the flesh without
damaging the skin. Reserve the skin.
5 Liquidise or mash half the melon flesh to
make melon purée. (Remaining melon can
be used in a fruit salad.)
6 Combine the remaining sugar syrup with
the melon purée, add the ginger and
sufficient green colouring to give a natural
melon colour. Pour the melon syrup and the
redcurrant syrup in separate shallow plastic
boxes. Freeze until semi-solid.
7 Whisk the egg white until stiff but not dry.
Whip the cream until softly stiff.
8 Turn each of the semi-solid fruit ices into a
bowl and mash, then add about ⅔ of the
whisked egg white to the melon ice followed
by ⅔ of the whipped cream and evenly fold
in. Add the remaining egg white and cream to

the redcurrant ice. Fold in. Return the iced creams to their boxes and freeze until almost solid.

9 Remove the melon iced cream from the freezer. Divide in half and work it with a fork to make it slightly soft then quickly spread a thick layer on the inside of each melon shell. Return to the freezer until firm.

10 Mash the redcurrant iced cream down a little and then when it is slightly soft spoon it into the centre of the melon shells to fill. If liked, press raisins or slivers of prune in neat rows in the red iced cream so when it is cut later they look like the black seeds of a watermelon.

11 Cover each melon half with cling film and freeze until completely solid.

12 Cut the melon into wedges just before serving. (They look good arranged on a plate decorated with dark shiny leaves.) Serve with Ginger Sauce.

Serves 6-8

Note: Canned raspberries may be used instead of the fresh fruit.

GINGER SAUCE

4 level tablespoons granulated sugar
8 tablespoons cold water
1 tablespoon lemon juice
6-8 pieces stem ginger, sliced
4 tablespoons syrup from jar of ginger

Gently dissolve the sugar in the water then boil steadily until it is syrupy. Add the lemon juice, ginger and syrup, stir. Serve when cold.

BROWN BETTY ICED CREAM

6 heaped tablespoons (40 g/1½ oz) fresh
  brown wholewheat breadcrumbs
75 g/3 oz demerara sugar
275 ml/10 fl oz fresh double cream
¼ teaspoon vanilla essence

1 Preheat the oven to 220°C/425°F/Gas 7.
2 Combine the crumbs and sugar in a sandwich tin and bake for about 10 minutes, stirring from time to time, until the sugar becomes sticky and starts to caramelise. Remove from the oven and cool.
3 Crush the caramelised crumbs with a rolling pin until very fine.
4 Whip the cream with the vanilla essence until softly stiff then fold in the crumbs.
5 Turn the mixture into 4 individual dishes, cover and freeze until firm. This iced cream is good served topped with apple purée and a scattering of raisins, or with sliced bananas, a little soured cream and some brown sugar crystals.

Serves 4-6

TUTTI FRUTTI BOMBE

Chocolate iced cream
3 egg yolks
50 g/2 oz caster sugar
1 level tablespoon custard powder
275 ml/½ pint milk
175 g/6 oz plain dessert chocolate
150 ml/5 fl oz fresh single cream
150 ml/5 fl oz fresh double cream
Orange iced cream
3 egg yolks
75 g/3 oz caster sugar
1 level tablespoon custard powder
150 ml/¼ pint milk
finely grated rind of 1 orange
150 ml/¼ pint orange juice
yellow food colouring
red food colouring
125 g/4 oz mixed glacé fruit, finely chopped
3 tablespoons orange liqueur
275 ml/10 fl oz fresh double cream
25 g/1 oz blanched almonds, chopped

1 Make the chocolate iced cream: mix the egg yolks in a basin with the sugar and custard powder. Slowly bring the milk to boiling point and when almost boiling stir it briskly into the egg mixture. Return this custard to a very low heat and stir until thick. Place a piece of cling film on the surface of the custard, to prevent a skin forming, then leave aside to cool.
2 Melt the chocolate with 3 tablespoons of the single cream by placing it in a basin resting over a pan of hot water. Stir the melted chocolate evenly into the cooled custard.
3 Whip the double cream with the remaining single cream until softly stiff then mix it smoothly into the cold chocolate custard.
4 Freeze the chocolate custard until it begins to stiffen round the edges. Beat well, then freeze again until very stiff.
5 Use a tablespoon to coat an oiled 1.75 litre/3 pint plastic pudding basin with the chocolate iced cream. The coating should be about 2 cm/¾ inch thick. If it becomes soft as you do this, freeze again so the iced cream hardens and is then easier to smooth to an even thickness. Return the basin to the freezer.
6 Make the orange iced cream: mix the egg yolks in a basin with the sugar and custard powder. Heat the milk and make a very thick custard as in stage 1. Stir in the orange rind and juice then stir over a medium heat until thick. Mix in 4 drops yellow and then about 3 drops red colouring or sufficient to make the custard an attractive orange colour. Leave the custard to cool.
7 Cover the chopped glacé fruit with the liqueur. Whip the double cream until softly stiff then fold it into the cold orange custard with the chopped nuts, glacé fruit and liqueur. Freeze until setting round the edges. Beat and freeze again until almost solid.
8 Spoon the orange iced cream into the chocolate-lined basin to fill the centre. Smooth level and freeze the bombe for several hours until solid.

9 When ready to serve, dip the basin in a bowl of hot water, run a knife round the edge and turn it on to a serving plate. Freeze iced cream to store, but allow to mellow at room temperature before serving.
Serves 10-12

AVOCADO ICED CREAM WITH BLACKCURRANT SAUCE

284 ml/10 fl oz fresh double cream
3 ripe avocados, halved and stoned
6 tablespoons lemon juice
3 egg whites
75 g/3 oz caster sugar
227-g/8-oz can blackcurrants
4 level tablespoons icing sugar, sifted
whipped cream (optional)
50 g/2 oz walnuts, chopped

1 Whip the double cream until softly stiff.
2 Spoon out the avocado flesh and mash with the lemon juice. Beat until smooth then fold in the cream.
3 Whisk the egg whites until very stiff then gradually whisk in the caster sugar so that the mixture is stiff and meringue-like.
4 Fold the egg whites very evenly into the avocado cream mixture then turn it into a 1.1 litre/2 pint container. Cover and freeze.
5 To make the sauce: press the blackcurrants through a sieve and stir in icing sugar to taste.
6 Place scoops of the avocado iced cream in individual dishes. Pour over the blackcurrant sauce, top with whipped cream if liked, then scatter with chopped walnuts.
Serves 8-10

Look No Cooker!

No-cook dishes to surprise everyone on a camping or caravan holiday or just when your cooker is having a day off!

TABBOULEH SALAD WITH FISH AND EGG

Bulgur wheat, obtainable from health food stores, is useful to keep in the store cupboard both for cold dishes, like this, and also hot ones, see pages 45 and 85. It does require very careful, almost heavy, seasoning to bring out the delicious nutty flavour.

225 g/8 oz bulgur wheat
4 tablespoons salad oil
2 tablespoons vinegar
3 tablespoons lemon juice
salt and freshly ground black pepper
4 well-rounded tablespoons chopped parsley
   or 1 level tablespoon dried parsley
4 level tablespoons chopped chives or 1 level
   tablespoon dried chives
1-2 tablespoons finely chopped fresh mint
225 g/8 oz onion, very finely chopped
½ lettuce, finely shredded
4 well rounded tablespoons mayonnaise
65 ml/2½ fl oz fresh single cream
185-g/6.53-oz can tuna, drained
2 hard-boiled eggs, quartered (optional)
¼ cucumber, diced
1 small green pepper, deseeded and sliced
   into rings
onion rings
25 g/1 oz black olives
2-3 tomatoes, quartered

1 Place the wheat in a bowl and cover with cold water. Leave aside for ½ hour to swell.
2 Combine the oil, vinegar and 2 tablespoons of the lemon juice in a bowl, then season lightly with salt and pepper. Stir in the parsley, chives and mint.

3 Drain the wheat in a fine sieve then turn it into a teatowel and squeeze out as much water as possible. Add the wheat to the bowl with the dressing, stir in the onion and mix well. Season further to taste.
4 Spread the shredded lettuce on a plate and pile the wheat salad on to it.
5 Combine the mayonnaise, cream and remaining lemon juice together. Season with salt and pepper then stir in the drained tuna, the quartered eggs and the diced cucumber.
6 Make a well in the wheat salad and spoon this fish mayonnaise into the centre. Scatter the top with the rings of green pepper and onion and then the black olives. Arrange the quartered tomatoes around the edge of the salad.
Serves 6

CAROL'S PARADISE CREAM

Avocados are good in puddings too! This creamy avocado pudding is even better topped with a layer of sliced and sugared strawberries, when in season.

1 large ripe avocado
2 tablespoons lemon juice
150 ml/5 fl oz fresh double cream
65 ml/2½ fl oz fresh single cream
3 level tablespoons caster sugar
2-3 rounded teaspoons creamed coconut (optional)
long strand coconut or sugared rose petals (optional)

1 Cut the avocado in half and remove the stone. Scoop the flesh into a bowl and mash with the lemon juice until smooth.
2 Whip both the creams with the sugar until softly stiff then stir in the avocado.
3 Mix the creamed coconut with 1 tablespoon boiling water until smoothly blended, then stir it into the avocado cream.
4 Spoon the cream mixture into 4 individual dishes and decorate, if liked, with long strand coconut or rose petals.
Serves 4

MURIEL'S PUDDING

150 ml/5 fl oz fresh double cream
225 g/8 oz full fat soft cheese
125 g/4 oz icing sugar, sifted
1 egg yolk
2 tablespoons brandy
toasted almonds or green grapes

1 Whip the cream until softly stiff.
2 Mix the cheese with the icing sugar and egg yolk. Fold in the whipped cream and the brandy until evenly blended.
3 Divide the mixture between 4-6 individual dishes and chill for at least 2 hours. Top with toasted almonds or halved and seeded green grapes to serve.
Serves 4-6

Good Travellers

Dishes to pack up and take with you for a picnic with a difference — be it a day on the beach or something grander.

CRUNCHY CHICKEN DRUMSTICKS WITH AVOCADO SAUCE

50 g/2 oz fresh breadcrumbs
50 g/2 oz shelled walnuts, minced or very
    finely chopped
50 g/2 oz English Cheddar cheese, finely
    grated
salt and pepper
40 g/1½ oz English butter, melted
1 clove garlic, crushed
8-12 chicken drumsticks

1 Preheat the oven to 180°C/350°F/Gas 4, shelf above centre.
2 Combine the breadcrumbs on a plate with the chopped walnuts and grated cheese; season well with salt and pepper.

3 Mix the butter with the crushed garlic and brush this over the drumsticks then dip them in the crumb mixture, pressing it well on to coat thickly.
4 Bake the chicken for about 35 minutes until cooked and the coating is crisp and golden. Serve with Avocado Sauce and perhaps an orange, onion and watercress salad.
Serves 4-6
Note: For a change, try the same crunchy coating on baked or grilled chicken or turkey breasts. Serve them hot with the cold sauce.

AVOCADO SAUCE

1 large avocado, halved and stoned
1 tablespoon lime or lemon juice
150 ml/5 fl oz soured cream
2 rounded tablespoons mayonnaise
½ level teaspoon dried basil
1 teaspoon Worcestershire sauce
salt and pepper

Spoon out the avocado flesh and mash smoothly with the lime or lemon juice then stir in the soured cream, mayonnaise, basil, Worcestershire sauce, salt and pepper to taste. Keep covered until required.

MIDDLE EAST LAMB SAUSAGES WITH CUCUMBER SALAD

Anyone who knows the Middle East would be horrified at my name for this dish – but it's the nearest description I can think of – and they are rather special sausages!

125 g/4 oz bulgur wheat
1 cucumber, thinly sliced
salt
225 g/8 oz onion
450 g/1 lb minced lamb
2 cloves garlic, crushed
pepper
25 g/1 oz English butter
2 tablespoons oil
½ level teaspoon dried mint
extra crushed garlic (optional)
150 ml/5 fl oz soured cream

1 Place the wheat in a bowl, cover with cold water and stand for 30 minutes, then drain well.
2 Lightly sprinkle the cucumber slices with salt and leave to drain in a colander.
3 Grate the onion into a bowl, add the minced lamb, drained wheat, garlic, salt and pepper to taste.
4 Knead the mixture together then divide equally and roll into 16 finger shapes.
5 Drain the cucumber well.
6 Fry the lamb fingers or sausages in the butter and oil until well browned. Remove and keep them hot.
7 Meanwhile, stir black pepper, mint and a little crushed garlic, if liked, into the soured cream. Add the drained cucumber.
8 Serve the lamb fingers hot or cold on a bed of lettuce, sprinkle with olive oil and lemon juice. Serve with the cucumber salad and, if available, sesame seed rolls.
Serves 4-6
Note: If you split pitta bread open to make a pouch, it can be stuffed with lettuce and these lamb fingers to make picnic sandwiches. Take the cucumber salad to ladle in just before eating.

SAVOURY SPREADS

These three spreads will each fill 4-6 rounds of sandwiches – and you won't need to butter the bread first. As the fillings will freeze they are useful to go in a batch of sandwiches to be kept, as a standby, in the freezer – ready for that spur of the minute journey or picnic or just a special packed lunch.

BACON AND MUSHROOM SANDWICH FILLING

125 g/4 oz streaky bacon, derinded and minced or finely chopped
125 g/4 oz mushrooms, minced or finely chopped
125 g/4 oz English butter
4 tablespoons fresh single or double cream
salt and pepper

Gently fry the bacon and mushrooms in the butter. Remove from the heat when cooked, cool slightly then stir in the cream, salt and pepper to taste. Turn the filling into a container, cover and chill until required.

CHEESE, ONION AND TOMATO PASTE

75 g/3 oz English Cheddar cheese, finely
   grated
25 g/1 oz onion, very finely chopped
125 g/4 oz tomato, peeled and finely chopped
50 g/2 oz English butter, melted
2 tablespoons fresh single or double cream
salt and pepper

Place the cheese in a bowl, stir in the onion, tomato, melted butter and cream. Beat the paste until smooth, season with salt and pepper to taste. Cover and chill until required.

NUT SPREAD

3 tablespoons peanut butter
125 g/4 oz full fat soft cheese
5-6 tablespoons fresh single or double cream
1 level teaspoon yeast extract

Mix together the peanut butter and cheese in a bowl. Stir in the cream and yeast extract. Cover and chill until required.

POTTED EGG WITH ANCHOVY

175 g/6 oz English butter
25 g/1 oz onion, very finely chopped
3 hard-boiled eggs
3-4 teaspoons anchovy essence (optional)
4 tablespoons fresh single cream
salt and pepper
1 tablespoon finely chopped parsley

1 Gently melt the butter, add the onion and cook very gently, without colouring, until soft.
2 Mash the eggs in a bowl and when very finely mashed mix in the onion and melted butter and anchovy essence, if liked.
3 Add the cream, salt and pepper to taste and the parsley.

4 Turn the mixture into an attractive container, smooth over and fork the top. Cover and chill until cold. Serve the potted egg with crusty brown bread and watercress or crisp rye biscuits. It may be refrigerated for storage but is best served at room temperature.
Serves 4-6

CHEESE AND ONION PIE

225 g/8 oz onion, finely chopped
25 g/1 oz English butter
1 egg (size 6)
75 g/3 oz fresh breadcrumbs
225 g/8 oz cottage cheese
2 tablespoons chopped chives
125 g/4 oz English Cheddar cheese, grated
65 ml/2½ fl oz fresh single cream
salt and pepper
370-g/13-oz packet frozen puff pastry, thawed

1 Gently fry the onion in the butter until it is soft but not coloured. Cool.
2 Beat the egg in a bowl (reserve a little for glazing). Add the breadcrumbs, cottage cheese, chives, grated cheese, cream and fried onion. Season very well with salt and pepper and mix until evenly blended. Leave aside.
3 Preheat the oven to 220°C/425°F/Gas 7, shelf above centre.
4 Roll the pastry to a rectangle about 30 x 36 cm/12 x 14 inch. Trim neatly. Fold the pastry lengthwise into 3. Slip the folded pastry on to a large baking sheet; unfold, spread the cheese mixture down the centre then cut 2.5 cm/1 inch strips towards the centre in the pastry on either side. Fold in 2.5 cm/1 inch pastry at ends over the filling then dampen strips and fold alternately over the cheese filling to give a plaited effect.
5 Glaze the top of the pie with the reserved beaten egg then bake for about 35 minutes until the pastry is cooked and golden. Serve hot or cold.
Serves 6

The Rule of the Waves

A special menu to make with the aid of a microwave cooker.

MUSHROOMS BEELZEBUB

225 g/8 oz mushrooms, thinly sliced
25 g/1 oz English butter
150 ml/5 fl oz fresh double cream
1 tablespoon Worcestershire sauce
1 tablespoon tomato ketchup
1 level teaspoon mustard powder
2 teaspoons lemon juice
½ level teaspoon curry powder
1 level teaspoon cornflour
salt and pepper
paprika

1 Place the sliced mushrooms and butter in an uncovered dish. Microwave on Full for 3 minutes or until cooked, stirring halfway through.
2 Blend together 125 ml/4 fl oz of the cream with the Worcestershire sauce, tomato ketchup, mustard powder, lemon juice, curry powder and cornflour. Stir together with the mushrooms then season well with salt and pepper.
3 Microwave on Defrost for about 3 minutes, or until hot. Take care not to allow the mixture to boil.
4 Divide this mixture equally between 4 little individual dishes (soufflé dishes are ideal) then microwave for 1 minute on Defrost until hot. Just before serving, top with a swirl of the remaining cream and a dusting of paprika.
Serves 4
Note: Output of microwave oven used – 700 watts.

FISH CREAM WITH PRAWN AND LEMON SAUCE

450 g/1 lb cod, filleted
2 eggs (size 1, 2), beaten
50 g/2 oz fresh breadcrumbs
50 g/2 oz onion, finely chopped or grated
150 ml/5 fl oz fresh single cream
salt and pepper
chopped parsley

1   Remove skin and bone from the fish and then mince flesh (process or liquidise) finely.
2   Mix in the eggs, breadcrumbs, onion and cream. Season to taste with salt and pepper.
3   Turn the fish mixture into a 1 litre/1¾ pint buttered soufflé dish or mould. Cover with cling film then microwave on Defrost for about 10 minutes or until set round the edge and coming away from the dish. Remove cling film. Leave to stand for 5 minutes until mixture feels firm in the centre. If it does not feel firm, cover again and return the dish to the microwave and cook on Defrost until it is firmer. Remove cling film.
4   Run a knife round the inside of the fish mould and carefully turn it out on to a plate. Spoon the Prawn and Lemon Sauce over it and top with a sprinkling of parsley to serve.
Serves 4-6
Note: Output of microwave oven used – 700 watts.

PRAWN AND LEMON SAUCE

2 level tablespoons cornflour
25 g/1 oz English butter
½ chicken stock cube
275 ml/½ pint milk
2 tablespoons lemon juice
125 g/4 oz shelled prawns
65 ml/2½ fl oz fresh single cream
salt and pepper

1   Mix the cornflour, butter, stock cube and milk in a glass measuring jug. Stir well then microwave on Full for 1 minute. Stir again.
2   Add the lemon juice and prawns. Microwave for a further 1 minute. Stir, cool slightly then mix in the cream and season to taste with salt and pepper.

CHOCOLATE MELODY

125 g/4 oz English butter, softened
125 g/4 oz caster sugar
2 eggs
90 g/3½ oz self-raising flour
15 g/½ oz cocoa powder
¼ teaspoon almond essence
425-g/15-oz can black cherries, drained and stoned
150 ml/5 fl oz fresh double cream
1 level tablespoon icing sugar, sifted

1   Beat the butter with the caster sugar, eggs, sifted flour and cocoa. After about 2 minutes when pale and creamy mix in the almond essence.
2   Spoon a little of the pudding mixture into a greased 1.5 litre/2½ pint pudding basin. Mix the drained cherries into the remaining mixture and pile into the basin. Smooth the top level and cover with cling film.
3   Microwave the pudding for about 5-6 minutes on Full (turning the basin every 3 minutes) until it is well risen with a slightly moist top. Remove cling film. Cool the pudding and turn on to a wire rack.
4   Whip the double cream with the icing sugar until stiff. When the pudding is cold, cut it into 3 layers horizontally and sandwich together again with the whipped cream. Serve the chocolate pudding with the Hot Chocolate Sauce.
Serves 6
Note: Output of microwave used – 700 watts.

HOT CHOCOLATE SAUCE

50 g/2 oz plain dessert chocolate
40 g/1½ oz caster sugar
65 ml/2½ fl oz fresh single cream

1   Break the chocolate into a basin, add the caster sugar, 2 tablespoons cold water and the single cream.
2   Microwave on Full for about 1½ minutes then whip with a balloon whisk or fork until the sauce is smooth and slightly thick.

Fishing for Compliments

When the fish finger reigns supreme and fishmongers are putting up their shutters, an unusual fish dish makes a good talking point. These recipes fit most occasions and can be varied in quantity to suit most appetites.

ROLLED SOUFFLÉ WITH PRAWNS AND MUSHROOMS

75 g/3 oz English butter
75 g/3 oz flour
425 ml/¾ pint milk
75 g/3 oz English Cheddar cheese, grated
3 eggs, separated
salt and pepper
grated nutmeg
Prawn and Mushroom Filling
225 g/8 oz mushrooms, sliced
50 g/2 oz English butter
40 g/1½ oz flour
150 ml/¼ pint milk
150 ml/5 fl oz fresh single cream
125 g/4 oz peeled prawns
salt and pepper
grated English Cheddar cheese to serve

1 Thoroughly grease a Swiss roll tin 20 x 30 cm/8 x 12 inches and line with greaseproof paper standing to a depth of 4 cm/1½ inches. Butter the paper well.
2 Melt the butter in a saucepan, mix in the flour then remove the pan from the heat and smoothly blend in the milk. Stir continuously over a medium heat until the mixture comes to the boil and is thick and smooth. Stir in the cheese. Cool.
3 Preheat the oven to 180°C/350°F/Gas 4, shelf above centre.
4 Stir the egg yolks into the sauce and season with salt, pepper and grated nutmeg to taste.
5 Whisk the egg whites very stiffly and then mix 2 tablespoons of them into the sauce. Gently fold in the remainder until evenly blended. Spread the mixture smoothly in the prepared Swiss roll tin and bake the soufflé for about 45 minutes or until it is well risen and golden topped.
6 Meanwhile for the filling, fry the sliced mushrooms in the butter. Remove the pan from the heat to stir in the flour then blend in the milk. Gently heat the sauce, stirring until it is very thick then stir in the cream and prawns. Season to taste.
7 Turn the cooked soufflé mixture out on to a large sheet of buttered foil, very carefully ease away the greaseproof paper then spread evenly with the filling. Carefully roll up the soufflé (like a Swiss roll) and serve immediately. If it is necessary to keep the

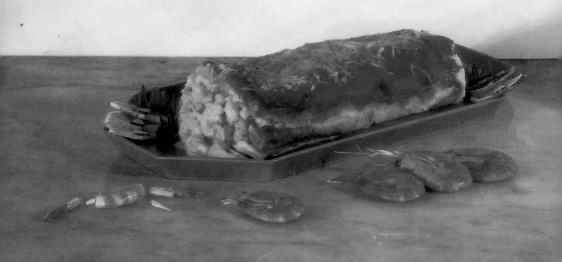

soufflé warm for any length of time, wrap in the foil until required.

8 To serve, place the roll on a plate. Dust thickly with grated cheese.

Serves 4-6

Note: This makes an impressive and filling lunch dish. It is the luck of the draw if you achieve a perfect roll – but don't worry, just scatter thickly with cheese to hide any faults! Fillings can be varied to suit your own taste; fish in a creamy sauce with spinach is good.

FISH AND RICE TIMBALE WITH CHEESE SAUCE

225 g/8 oz onion, chopped finely
75 g/3 oz English butter
175 g/6 oz long grain rice
575 ml/1 pint chicken stock
1 egg, beaten
salt and pepper
50 g/2 oz flour
575 ml/1 pint milk, or milk and fish stock
225 g/8 oz smoked cod, cooked and flaked
300-g/10.6-oz packet cut leaf spinach, thawed
2 large tomatoes, peeled
75 g/3 oz English Cheddar cheese, grated
65 ml/2½ fl oz fresh single cream

1 Fry the onion until soft in 25 g/1 oz of the butter then stir in the rice and stock. Bring to the boil, then reduce the heat, cover the pan, and gently simmer for about 20 minutes until all the liquid has been absorbed and the rice is cooked. Stir in the beaten egg and season with salt and pepper.

2 Melt the remaining butter in a saucepan, stir in the flour then remove from the heat to blend in 425 ml/¾ pint of the milk or milk and fish stock. Stir the sauce continuously over a medium heat until thick. Turn half the sauce into a bowl and stir in the smoked fish. Season to taste.

3 Layer ⅓ of the rice, ½ the spinach, ½ the fish mixture and a sliced tomato in a 1.75 litre/3 pint pudding basin. Repeat the layers finishing with an extra layer of rice.

4 Cover the basin with foil and steam for 20 minutes until hot. Add the remaining 150 ml/¼ pint milk and the cheese to the sauce, then stir over a medium heat until the cheese has melted. Cool slightly then stir in the cream and season to taste.

5 Turn the timbale out on to a hot serving plate and serve with the sauce.

Serves 4 as a complete meal

CRISPY-TOPPED SEAFOOD PIE

A pie that can be served for brunch, lunch, tea or supper!

190 g/6½ oz English butter
250 g/9 oz flour
275 ml/½ pint milk
1 small onion, sliced
1 bayleaf
1 blade of mace
150 ml/5 fl oz fresh single cream
227-g/8-oz can salmon
4 hard-boiled eggs, chopped
125 g/4 oz peeled prawns
2 teaspoons anchovy essence
salt and pepper
2 eggs, beaten
50 g/2 oz English Cheddar cheese, grated

1   Rub 125 g/4 oz of the butter into 175 g/6 oz of the flour. Bind the pastry together with about 1 tablespoon cold water. Chill.
2   Preheat the oven to 200°C/400°F/Gas 6, shelf above centre. Roll the pastry out to line a 25 cm/10 inch flan tin or dish. Line with paper towel and baking beans then bake for about 15 minutes, remove the paper and beans then continue to cook for about 15-20 minutes until the pastry is crisp. Remove the pastry shell from oven then increase the heat to 220°C/425°F/Gas 7.
3   Meanwhile very gently heat the milk in a covered saucepan with the sliced onion, bayleaf and mace for about 30 minutes. Strain.
4   Melt 25 g/1 oz of the butter in a saucepan, mix in 25 g/1 oz of the flour then remove from the heat to blend in the strained milk. Stir the sauce over a medium heat, until it comes to the boil then remove from the heat and cool slightly before stirring in the cream.
5   Remove the black skin and bones from the salmon then add, with its juice, to the sauce. Stir in the chopped hard-boiled eggs and prawns, season with anchovy essence, salt and freshly ground black pepper to taste. Spoon the sauce into the pastry shell.
6   Sift the remaining 50 g/2 oz flour with a pinch of salt. Measure the remaining 40 g/1½ oz butter into a saucepan with 125 ml/4 fl oz water then slowly bring to the boil. Remove from the heat and immediately add the flour, all at once. Beat with a wooden spoon until the mixture leaves the sides of the pan cleanly. Cool slightly then beat in the eggs until the mixture is smooth and shiny.
7   Spoon this choux paste round the edge of the flan or pipe it in a thin trellis pattern.
8   Scatter the pie with cheese and bake for about 35-40 minutes until the choux paste is puffed up and golden.
Serves 8

FISH WITH EGG AND GRAPEFRUIT SAUCE

6 small cod fillets
flour
salt and pepper
125 g/4 oz English butter
3 tablespoons oil
2 hard-boiled eggs
6 tablespoons fresh double cream
½ grapefruit (6 tablespoons grapefruit juice)
1 level tablespoon chopped chives

1 Season the flour and use it to coat the fish.
2 Melt half the butter with the oil in a large frying pan then fry the fish over a medium heat for about 10 minutes.
3 Meanwhile, gently melt the remaining 50 g/2 oz butter in a saucepan. Mash the eggs with a fork and add to the butter with the cream, grapefruit juice and chives. Season to taste with salt and pepper then simmer over a higher heat until slightly thick.
4 Arrange the cooked fish on a hot serving plate and coat with some of the Egg and Grapefruit Sauce. Serve the rest separately.
Serves 6

Sunday Best

The following recipes served with a joint make the traditional 'roast' into something special.

SOUPE VERTE

A pretty soup with a delicate flavour of summer. It can be served hot or cold.

50 g/2 oz English butter
125 g/4 oz onion, finely chopped
225 g/8 oz potatoes, peeled and chopped
1 bunch of watercress, coarsely chopped
½ cucumber (about 225 g/8 oz), peeled and diced
the outside leaves of a lettuce (about 125 g/4 oz), shredded
1 level tablespoon flour
125 g/4 oz frozen peas
425 ml/¾ pint stock or water plus 1 chicken stock cube
425 ml/¾ pint milk
salt and pepper
65 ml/2½ fl oz fresh single cream

1 Melt the butter in a saucepan and fry the onion and potatoes gently until softening but not coloured; stir from time to time. Add the watercress, cucumber and shredded lettuce and fry very gently for a further 5 minutes, turning frequently.
2 Sprinkle the lightly cooked vegetables with the flour. Cook for a further minute then add the peas and mix in the stock. Simmer for 30 minutes.
3 Purée the soup, add the milk and return to the saucepan. Season the soup to taste, bring slowly to the boil then remove the pan from the heat to cool slightly before stirring in the cream.
Serves 6-8
Note: When sorrel is in season a couple of chopped sorrel leaves may be added to the vegetables to give the soup a delicate lemon flavour.

SPINACH CASSEROLE

675 g/1½ lb fresh spinach or two 225-g/8-oz packets frozen chopped spinach, thawed
125 g/4 oz mushrooms, chopped (optional)
125 g/4 oz onion, chopped
50-75 g/2-3 oz English butter
4 tablespoons fresh single cream
salt and pepper
grated nutmeg
50 g/2 oz fresh white breadcrumbs
½ level teaspoon dried rosemary (optional)

1 Preheat the oven to 180°C/350°F/Gas 4, shelf above centre.
2 Blanch the *fresh* spinach, drain and chop. Now put the blanched *fresh* spinach or the thawed spinach in a bowl.
3 Fry the mushrooms and onion in the butter until cooked and lightly brown. This will take about 5 minutes. Remove them with a draining spoon and add to the spinach with the cream, salt and pepper and grated nutmeg to taste. Turn the mixture into a greased 850 ml/1½ pint ovenproof dish.
4 Add the crumbs, mixed with the rosemary if using, to the fat in the pan and quickly stir over a medium heat until crisp but not golden, then sprinkle them over the spinach.

5 Bake the spinach casserole for about 20 minutes until piping hot.

Serves 6-8

Note: For a change, thinly slivered anchovies arranged in a trellis on top of the crumbs before baking look attractive and go very well with roast lamb. This casserole also makes a good supper dish if you fry about 125 g/4 oz bacon with the onion.

SCANDINAVIAN ROAST POTATOES

6-8 even-sized large potatoes
50 g/2 oz English butter
4 tablespoons fresh single cream
salt
2 rounded tablespoons fresh breadcrumbs
1 clove garlic, crushed (optional)
50 g/2 oz English Cheddar cheese, finely
    grated

1 Peel the potatoes and trim so that they are evenly sized and stand firmly without rolling.
2 Cut the potatoes almost through (to within 1.5 cm/½ inch of the base) as though you were cutting them in 5 mm/¼ inch slices.

This job is made easier if you rest the potato to be cut on a wooden spoon.
3 Place the partially sliced potatoes in a bowl and cover with cold water.
4 Preheat the oven to 220°C/425°F/Gas 7, centre shelf.
5 Thickly grease a shallow baking dish with the butter.
6 Lift the potatoes from the water, pat them dry and arrange, cut side up, in the baking dish. Brush each one with cream, sprinkle liberally with salt and place to cook.
7 Mix the crumbs into the remaining cream. Stir in the garlic, if using. After the potatoes have been cooking for 30 minutes, spoon the butter in the dish over them then scatter with the crumbs and cook for a further 15 minutes.
8 Pierce the potatoes to check they are cooked; if not, reduce the oven temperature to 190°C/375°F/Gas 5; baste with butter from the dish and continue cooking until they are golden brown and tender.
9 Scatter the potatoes with the cheese before the final 10 minutes of cooking.
Serves 6-8

Children's Party Cakes

Cakes designed to bring out those 'oohs' and 'aahs' at the right time.

PRINCESS DIANA CAKE

50 g/2 oz fudge, chopped
65 ml/2½ fl oz fresh single cream
50 g/2 oz chocolate chips
225 g/8 oz English butter, softened
225 g/8 oz caster sugar
4 eggs, beaten
275 g/10 oz self-raising flour
1 level teaspoon baking powder
6 tablespoons milk or warm water
Decoration
75 g/3 oz English butter, softened
1 tablespoon warm water
175 g/6 oz icing sugar, sifted
½ teaspoon vanilla essence
silver cake board (optional)
a small doll
doilys
ribbon
150 ml/5 fl oz fresh double cream, whipped
silver balls
tulle for veil
ring for headdress
small posy of fresh or artificial flowers

1 Preheat the oven to 160°C/325°F/Gas 3, centre shelf. Grease a 2 litre/3½ pint ovenproof glass basin and line the base with a circle of greased greaseproof paper.

2 Place the chopped fudge and 3 tablespoons of the single cream in a bowl resting over a pan of simmering water. Stir until the fudge is melted to a creamy consistency. Cool. Now place the chocolate chips in a bowl with 3 tablespoons of single cream and heat over hot but *not* boiling water. Stir until the chocolate has melted to a creamy consistency. Cool.

3 Cream the butter and sugar until soft and creamy, beat in the eggs gradually. Sift the flour and baking powder then fold into the creamed mixture with the milk or water. Swirl in the fudge liquid and then the chocolate liquid, mixing so that they are only swirled in and not fully mixed in.

4 Spoon the cake mixture into the basin, level the surface and bake for 1¼-1½ hours until the centre of the cake feels firm when lightly pressed. If the top of the cake seems to be browning too quickly, cover with a piece of greaseproof paper.

5 Leave the cake in the bowl for 5 minutes then turn out on to a wire rack. Remove the lining paper and leave to cool.

6 Make the butter icing by creaming the butter with 1 tablespoon hot water and the icing sugar. Stir well then beat well until smooth. Add the vanilla essence. Spread the icing over the cake to coat it then place the cake on a plate or board.

7 Press the doll into the top of the cake so that the cake becomes the skirt of the doll. 'Dress' the top of the doll with folded doilys to make a lacy bodice then tie a ribbon round the waist to hide the seam between the doily bodice and the iced skirt. Pipe or spoon the whipped cream round the bottom and mark with a fork so that it looks like flounces round the bottom of the skirt. Decorate with silver balls. Arrange the headdress and veil on the doll and give her a posy of flowers.

TIMMY MOUSE CAKE

350 g/12 oz digestive biscuits
5 rounded tablespoons golden syrup
200 g/7 oz English butter
75 g/3 oz caster sugar
5 level tablespoons cocoa powder, sifted
75 g/3 oz crispy rice cereal
75 g/3 oz raisins (optional)
175 g/6 oz chocolate cake covering
2 dried apricots
225 ml/8 fl oz fresh double cream
1 stick of liquorice
3 chocolate beans

1 Put the biscuits in a polythene bag and roll with a rolling pin to crumb them.

2 Gently heat the syrup, butter and caster sugar together until melted. Then stir in the cocoa.

3 Put the cereal in a bowl. Stir in 1/3 of the cocoa mixture and the raisins, if using.

4 Stir the biscuit crumbs into the remaining cocoa mixture.

5 Combine the crumb and cereal mixtures together. Stir and leave to cool.

6 Turn the cooled mixture on to a baking sheet and mould with your hands to a long oval shape with a slight hump at one end and a point at the other. Cover with cling film and chill until firmly set.

7 Melt the chocolate in a bowl over hot (not boiling) water. Coat the mouse with a thin layer all over the body. Chill, and when hard slip the mouse body on to a cake board.

8 Press the dried apricots to mouse ear shapes then dip them in the melted chocolate and place aside to harden.

9 Whip the cream until stiff then fold in the remaining cooled melted chocolate. Spread this all over the mouse, then mark it with a fork to look like smooth fur. Press the liquorice into the rear end of the mouse for a tail, then insert the ears, two chocolate beans as eyes and one as a nose. Use a very sharp knife to cut thin slivers of liquorice as whiskers and press these in either side of the nose.

JOLLY SNOWMAN CAKE

225 g/8 oz English butter
125 g/4 oz caster sugar
100 g/4 oz soft brown sugar
4 eggs
225 g/8 oz self-raising flour
2 tablespoons instant coffee powder
2 teaspoons mixed spice
4 tablespoons milk
25 g/1 oz chocolate drops (optional)
50 g/2 oz sultanas
50 g/2 oz mixed peel
50 g/2 oz glacé cherries, quartered

Decoration
2 teaspoons caster sugar
3 tablespoons top of milk
284 ml/½ pint fresh double cream
50 g/2 oz long strand shredded coconut
2 chocolate buttons
1 icecream cone or piece of carrot
strip of red bootlace liquorice
stick of black liquorice (optional)
1 chocolate digestive biscuit
1 chocolate-coated marshmallow
piece of fabric to make scarf

1 Heat the oven to 180°C, 350°F, Gas 4, centre shelf. Butter a 1.5 litre/2½ pint oven glass pudding basin and a 300 ml/½ pint oven glass measuring jug. Line the base of each with a small disc of buttered greaseproof paper.
2 Cream the butter and caster sugar together until soft and fluffy. Add the soft brown sugar and continue beating until mixture is much paler and soft and creamy.
3 Beat the eggs and add by degrees to the cake mixture, beating well after each addition.
4 Sift the flour with the coffee powder and mixed spice then add to the mixture with the milk. Stir well until evenly blended. Mix in the chocolate dots, sultanas, mixed peel and glacé cherries.
5 Spoon the mixture into the prepared containers.
6 Bake the cakes until pale golden and firm to a light touch, allowing about 40 minutes for the measuring jug and 1 hour 10 minutes

for the pudding basin.
7 When the cakes are cooked, cool them slightly then slip a knife round the edge of each and carefully turn them on to a rack.
8 When the cakes are cold, stand the smaller cake on top of the larger one to make the head and body of the snowman.
9 Add caster sugar to taste and the top of the milk to the cream. Whip until softly thick.
10 Spread the cream all over the snowman to coat completely then scatter evenly with the long strand coconut.
11 Press the chocolate buttons on the face as eyes. Cut off the pointed end of the icecream cone or use a piece of carrot for a nose. Cut a strip of liquorice into a smiling mouth and press in place.
12 If you like, make a pipe from the black liquorice. Cut a piece about 5 cm/2 inches long for the stem, and a piece about 1 cm/½ inch for the bowl. Fix the pieces together, using the end of a toothpick to pin them. Press the pipe into the cake just above the snowman's mouth.
13 Place the digestive biscuit, chocolate-side up, on the head at a rakish angle and top with the chocolate-coated marshmallow to make a hat.
14 Finally tie the scarf round the snowman's neck to keep him warm!
Note: Besides being suitable for a winter birthday cake this recipe also makes an alternative to the traditional Christmas cake. For children, the fruit and peel can be left out. You can use any suitable ovenproof container to make a rough snowman shape. Then, when you swirl the cream on, you can use it to give the right effect.

Long strand shredded coconut is generally available at health food shops.

THREE BEARS' CAKE

225 g/8 oz self-raising flour
2 level teaspoons baking powder
225 g/8 oz caster sugar
225 g/8 oz English butter, softened
4 eggs
4 tablespoons milk
1 tablespoon finely grated lemon rind
   (optional)
450 g/1 lb modelling icing (see below)
blue or red food colouring
150 ml/5 fl oz fresh double cream, whipped
lemon curd or apricot jam
rice paper
3 small teddy bears (graded in size)
candles (optional)

1 Grease and line a 20 cm/8 inch (by 6 cm/2½ inches deep) square cake tin. Preheat the oven to 180°C/350°F/Gas 4, shelf above centre.
2 Sift the flour and baking powder into a mixing bowl, add the caster sugar, soft butter, eggs and milk. Mix ingredients well together then beat for about 3 minutes or until mixture is fluffy and paler in colour. Mix in the lemon rind, if using.
3 Spread the cake mixture smoothly in the prepared tin then bake for about 40 minutes until pale golden and firm to a light touch.
4 Cool the cake in the tin for about 15 minutes then turn it out on to a wire rack and leave until cold.

5 Roll ¾ of the icing out to about a 26 cm/10 inch square. Dip a clean paint brush in blue or red food colouring and paint a checked pattern and border on the fondant to make a bedspread. Roll the remaining icing out to a rectangle about 20 x 10 cm/8 x 4 inches and paint a matching border round the edge to act as a bolster cover, if liked.
6 Cut the cake into 3 layers and sandwich them together again with whipped cream and lemon curd (or apricot jam). Trim the cake neatly with a sharp knife and place on a cake board.
7 Place a sheet of rice paper on top of the cake then roll up another piece and place it at the top end to make a pillow. Cover with the icing bolster cover.
8 Arrange the 3 teddies on the 'bed'. Cover their bodies with rice paper, for protection, and then the icing bedspread.
9 If liked, arrange candles along the back of the 'bed' to look like a bedhead or at the 4 corners to make a fourposter.
Note: To make modelling icing, mix 50 g/2 oz liquid glucose with 1 egg white, using a wooden spoon. Stir until evenly blended. Gradually work in about 450 g/1 lb sifted icing sugar to form a firm, non-sticky 'dough'. Turn out on to a board dusted with cornflour and knead until smooth. Wrap in cling film and refrigerate until required.

Cream Teas

Special cakes to make a teatime centrepiece.

GOOEY CHOCOLATE CAKE WITH STRAWBERRIES

125 g/4 oz plain dessert chocolate
125 g/4 oz English butter, at room
    temperature
125 g/4 oz caster sugar
3 eggs, separated
50 g/2 oz ground almonds
¼ teaspoon almond essence
50 g/2 oz plain flour
225-275 ml/8-10 fl oz fresh double cream
sifted icing sugar
350-450 g/12 oz-1 lb strawberries

1 Preheat the oven to 180°C/350°F/Gas 4,
centre shelf. Grease a 20 cm/8 inch
springform cake tin and dust with caster
sugar.
2 Place 2 tablespoons water and break the
chocolate into a basin resting over a pan of
hot water. Heat very gently until the
chocolate has melted. Cool.
3 Meanwhile cream the butter with the
sugar until it is very soft, fluffy and paler in
colour. Beat in the egg yolks, one at a time,
beating well after each yolk is added.
4 Whisk the egg whites until very stiff.
5 Fold the melted chocolate into the
creamed mixture then the ground almonds
and almond essence.
6 Fold in a rounded tablespoon of the
whisked egg whites then mix in the flour, and
finally, fold in the remaining whisked whites
until all evenly blended. Spread the mixture
lightly and smoothly into the prepared tin.
7 Bake the cake for about 35 minutes or
until the outer edge is firm and springy but
the very centre of the cake remains slightly
soft.
8 Cool the cake slightly in the tin then turn it
out on to a wire rack and leave until cold.
9 Whip the cream with about 1 tablespoon
icing sugar until softly stiff.
10 Either serve the cake just dusted with
icing sugar and with a bowl of the whipped
cream and the strawberries to dollop on each
portion or, cut the cake carefully into 3 layers
then sandwich together again with sliced,
sugared strawberries and whipped cream,
reserving the best 5-6 strawberries and some
cream to decorate the top.
Note: The secret of this delicious gooey cake
simply lies in taking great care not to cook it
right through to the centre. Instead of
strawberries it's also good with grapes or
canned mandarin oranges.

GINGER, CINNAMON AND APPLE CAKE

75 g/3 oz caster sugar
75 g/3 oz soft brown sugar
125 g/4 oz English butter, at room
    temperature
225 g/8 oz plain flour
2 level teaspoons baking powder
½ level teaspoon salt
1 level teaspoon ground cinnamon
1 level teaspoon ground ginger
2 eggs
225 g/8 oz dessert apples, peeled and coarsely
    grated
4 pieces of stem ginger, chopped
50 g/2 oz raisins
2 tablespoons milk (optional)
caster sugar to dust
150 ml/5 fl oz fresh double cream
8 brandy snaps
8 small pieces of stem ginger for decoration

1 Preheat the oven to 180°C/350°F/Gas 4,
centre shelf. Grease and flour a 23 cm/9 inch
springform cake tin. A flan or sandwich tin
can be used instead provided it is 4 cm/
1½ inches deep.
2 Cream the sugars with the butter until soft
and much paler in colour.
3 Sift the flour with the baking powder, salt
and spices.
4 Gradually beat the eggs into the creamed
mixture then fold in the sieved flour.
5 Stir in the apples, ginger and raisins.
6 The cake mixture should be fairly soft, if
not stir in 1-2 tablespoons milk. Turn the cake
mixture into the prepared tin, smooth level
and bake for 30-40 minutes until firm to a
light touch.
7 Leave the cake in the tin to cool slightly
then turn out on to a wire rack and cool.
8 To decorate, dust the top of the cake with a
little caster sugar, whip the cream until softly
stiff and spoon a little into the ends of each of
the brandy snaps. Arrange these in a circle on
top of the cake. Pipe whirls of cream in
between each brandy snap and top this with
a small piece of stem ginger.

PASSION CAKE

This is my version of a cake which originated,
I think, in Canada. I've no idea why it is called
Passion Cake or indeed, what passion it's
meant to arouse!

125 g/4 oz plain flour
1 level teaspoon baking powder
¾ level teaspoon bicarbonate of soda
½ level teaspoon salt
1½ level teaspoons ground cinnamon
65 g/2½ oz caster sugar
125 ml/4 fl oz oil
2 eggs
50 g/2 oz carrot, finely grated
50 g/2 oz raisins
50 g/2 oz walnuts, chopped
200-g/7-oz can crushed pineapple, drained
2-3 tablespoons apricot jam

Topping
65 ml/2½ fl oz fresh double cream
50 g/2 oz icing sugar, sifted
75 g/3 oz full fat soft cheese
½ teaspoon vanilla essence
finely chopped walnuts to decorate

1 Preheat the oven to 180°C/350°F/Gas 4, centre shelf.
2 Sift the dry ingredients into a mixing bowl.
3 Add the sugar, oil and eggs. Mix well together.
4 Stir in the grated carrot, raisins, walnuts and drained pineapple.
5 Stir the mixture until evenly blended then turn it into a 20 cm/8 inch lined cake tin (preferably springform). Spread the mixture evenly in the tin then bake for 45 minutes to 1 hour or until it feels firm to a light touch in the centre.

6 Leave the cake to cool in the tin, then turn out and coat with apricot jam.
7 To make the topping: whip the cream until softly stiff, place aside. Cream the icing sugar and cheese together; add the vanilla essence then fold in the cream until smoothly blended.
8 Spread this cream cheese mixture evenly over the top and sides of the cake with a palette knife. Use the knife to make a slightly rough, swirling pattern in the icing. Finally, sprinkle chopped walnuts over the top of the cake.

SWISS-STYLE CHEESECAKE

Cheesecake filling
3 level teaspoons gelatine (15 g/
  ½ oz envelope)
3 tablespoons lemon juice
225 g/8 oz cottage cheese
125 g/4 oz full fat soft cheese
finely grated rind of ½ lemon
2 eggs, separated
125 g/4 oz caster sugar
150 ml/5 fl oz fresh double cream
50-75 g/2-3 oz raisins

Sponge cake
75 g/3 oz plain flour
1 level teaspoon baking powder
¼ teaspoon salt
3 egg yolks
75 g/3 oz caster sugar
4 tablespoons boiling water
1 teaspoon vanilla essence
1 teaspoon finely grated lemon rind
lemon curd or apricot jam
sifted icing sugar

1 Lightly oil a 20 cm/8 inch springform cake tin.

2 Measure the gelatine into a cup and stir in the lemon juice and 3 tablespoons cold water. Leave aside for 5 minutes to swell, then place the cup in a pan of hot water and heat gently until the gelatine melts. Cool slightly.

3 Sieve the cottage cheese through a metal sieve into a bowl and add the soft cheese, lemon rind and egg yolks. Mix together and stir in the gelatine (alternatively, to save sieving the cottage cheese, use a food processor to blend ingredients together).

4 Whisk the egg whites until very stiff then add the sugar gradually, whisking well after each addition.

5 Whip the cream until softly stiff.

6 Fold the cream, raisins and then the whisked egg whites into the gelatine mixture until evenly blended.

7 Turn the cheesecake mixture into the prepared tin and refrigerate until firmly set.

8 Meanwhile make the sponge cake: preheat the oven to 180°C/350°F/Gas 4, shelf above centre. Grease and line a 20 cm/8 inch sandwich tin.

9 Sift the flour with the baking powder and salt.

10 Whisk the egg yolks in a large bowl until very thick, foamy and mousse-like. Then, whisking, add the caster sugar a tablespoon at a time; whisk well after each addition until the mixture is pale and thick.

11 Carefully mix in the water, vanilla essence and lemon rind, then gently fold in the flour mixture until evenly blended.

12 Spread the cake mixture in the prepared tin and bake for about 25 minutes until it is well risen and firm to a light touch.

13 Leave the cake in the tin to cool for about 10 minutes then turn out on to a wire rack and leave until cold.

14 Cut the cake in half; place each layer, cut side up, on a worktop and spread fairly thickly with lemon curd or apricot jam.

15 Remove the set cheesecake from the tin

and sandwich between the sponge layers. Dust the top *very* thickly with icing sugar and, using the back of a long knife, mark a trellis pattern in the sugar.
Serves 8-10
Note: The sponge casing in this recipe makes a pleasant change from the more usual crumb crust used for cheesecakes. You may also find it a useful recipe to have to add to your repertoire of 'how to use up egg yolks'! However, if using the sponge for a cake use an 18 cm/7 inch sandwich tin.

CRISPY CHOCOLATE TARTLETS

1 rounded tablespoon golden syrup
25 g/1 oz English butter
75 g/3 oz plain dessert chocolate
50 g/2 oz crispy rice cereal

150 ml/5 fl oz fresh double cream
2-3 rounded tablespoons ginger conserve or canned crushed pineapple
grated chocolate (optional)

1 Measure the golden syrup, butter and chocolate into a saucepan and heat very gently until all melted. Stir together until smoothly blended.
2 Remove the pan from the heat, stir in the cereal until evenly coated with the syrup mixture.
3 Divide coated cereal between 12 bun tins and pat into shape to form little cases. Refrigerate until firmly set.
4 Whip the cream until softly stiff and fold in the ginger conserve or well drained crushed pineapple. Divide this mixture between the chocolate crispy tartlets and served chilled, dusted if liked with more grated chocolate.
Makes 12

Naughty But Nice!

*Irresistible cakes and desserts
that will tempt even the strictest
weight watcher!*

PINEAPPLE AND CHOCOLATE RING GÂTEAU

65 ml/2½ fl oz fresh single cream
65 ml/2½ fl oz cooking oil
125 g/4 oz self-raising flour
½ level teaspoon baking powder
125 g/4 oz caster sugar
2 eggs
finely grated rind of ½ lemon
½ level teaspoon gelatine
1 level tablespon icing sugar, sifted
150 ml/5 fl oz fresh double cream
75 g/3 oz chocolate cake covering
5 slices canned pineapple, drained

1 Preheat the oven to 160°C/325°F/Gas 3, centre shelf. Lightly brush a 575 ml/1 pint ring mould or an 18 cm/7 inch sandwich tin with oil.
2 Place the single cream, oil, flour, baking powder, caster sugar, eggs and lemon rind into a mixing bowl. Beat together until smoothly blended.
3 Turn the mixture into the prepared tin and bake for about 40 minutes or until golden and springy to the touch. Cool cake slightly in the tin then turn out on to a wire rack and leave until cold.
4 Place the gelatine in a basin, stir in 1 teaspoon cold water, leave for a few seconds then stir in 1 tablespoon boiling water to melt the gelatine. When cool, add the icing sugar and then the double cream. Beat until thick.
5 Melt the chocolate cake covering in a basin resting over a pan of hot water.
6 Cut the cake in half horizontally. Coat the top half of the cake with melted chocolate and leave to set.
7 Cut 1 slice of pineapple into 6 equal pieces and cut the remaining slices in half.
8 Pipe or spoon 6 rounds of cream on top of the chocolate coated cake half. Decorate each with a small piece of pineapple.
9 Arrange the remaining pieces of pineapple on the bottom layer of cake and pipe or spoon over the remaining cream. Top with the chocolate coated layer.
Cuts into 6 slices

CHARLOTTE MALAKOFF

275 ml/10 fl oz fresh double cream
175 g/6 oz English butter
175 g/6 oz caster sugar
75 g/3 oz ground almonds
75 g/3 oz fine cake crumbs
½ teaspoon almond essence
18 langues de chat or sponge finger biscuits
toasted flaked almonds (optional)

1 Grease a 15 cm/6 inch loose-based cake tin. Line with a round of greaseproof paper.
2 Whip the cream until softly stiff. Chill.
3 Cream the butter with the sugar until soft and fluffy then fold in the ground almonds, cake crumbs, almond essence and ⅔ of the whipped cream. Mix together until evenly blended.
4 Turn the almond mixture into the prepared cake tin; smooth level, cover with cling film then chill until firm.
5 Slip a knife round the edge of the charlotte to free it from the tin then turn it out on to a serving plate.
6 Trim the langues de chat or sponge finger biscuits to the same depth as the charlotte, then seal them round the sides with a little cream. Tie in place with a ribbon.
7 Pipe or spread the remaining cream on top of the charlotte and scatter with toasted almonds, if liked.
Serves 8

SPICED ORANGE AND CHOCOLATE ROLL

150 ml/5 fl oz fresh double cream
¼ level teaspoon ground cinnamon
2 level tablespoons brown sugar
2 level teaspoons finely grated orange rind
3 tablespoons orange juice
15 chocolate, nut and spice biscuits
additional whipped cream, chocolate and orange slices (optional)

1 Whip the cream until stiff with the cinnamon and sugar. Stir in the orange rind and juice and mix together until softly stiff.
2 Sandwich the biscuits together, with half the flavoured cream, to form a roll, then coat with remaining cream.
3 Place the biscuit roll on a plate, cover with cling film and refrigerate overnight.
4 Before serving, fork a pattern over the cream coating, and, if liked, pipe or spoon more whipped cream along the spine of the cake and decorate with chocolate and sliced orange.
5 To serve, cut the cake in diagonal slices.

ROLLED WALNUT SPONGE CAKE

To make this cake even naughtier, sprinkle it with rum or brandy to taste and then layer thinly sliced banana over the cream before rolling.

3 eggs (size 1, 2)
100 g/4 oz caster sugar
75 g/3 oz flour
¼ level teaspoon salt
65 g/2½ oz walnuts, finely chopped or minced
2 level teaspoons instant coffee powder
275 ml/10 fl oz fresh double cream
4 level tablespoons demerara sugar
sifted icing sugar

1 Preheat the oven to 200°C/400°F/Gas 6, shelf above centre.
2 Grease and line a Swiss roll tin about 23 x 33 cm/9 x 13 inches with greaseproof or non-stick kitchen paper.
3 Whisk the eggs in a bowl until they are very thick and mousse-like. Continue whisking, adding the sugar a little at a time. Whisk well after each addition until all the sugar is used up. Whisk again.
4 Working quickly, spoon half the mixture into another bowl, sift in the flour with the salt then gently fold together until evenly blended. Stir in 50 g/2 oz of the nuts.
5 Fold the remaining whisked eggs into the cake mixture, cutting it in gently but quickly, then spread evenly into the prepared tin.
6 Bake the cake for about 10 minutes or until it is evenly risen and pale golden and feels set to a light touch.
7 Spread a damp teatowel on a worktop, cover this with a piece of cling film sprinkled with caster sugar and turn the cooked cake on to it. Cool and trim the edges.
8 Dissolve the instant coffee in a bowl with 2 teaspoons boiling water. When cold, stir in the cream and demerara sugar; whip together until stiff.
9 Carefully remove the greaseproof or non-stick paper from the cake then spread over the whipped coffee cream.
10 Roll up the cake and wrap in the cling film to hold in place. Refrigerate until required.
11 Before serving unwrap the cake, sprinkle with the remaining 15 g/½ oz chopped walnuts then dust thickly with icing sugar.
Cuts into 8-10 slices
Note: This should be a failproof whisked sponge but, to avoid breaking your arm with all the whisking, use an electric or rotary mixer to do the work for you.

COFFEE BRANDY DESSERT GÂTEAU

5 level teaspoons instant coffee powder
5 level tablespoons icing sugar, sifted
2 tablespoons brandy
150 ml/5 fl oz fresh double cream
24 boudoir biscuits (sponge fingers)
whipped cream and toasted almonds to decorate

1 Place the instant coffee in a jug, add 3 tablespoons boiling water, stir until dissolved then add 2 tablespoons cold water.
2 Measure 1 tablespoon of this coffee into a basin and add 2 tablespoons icing sugar, 1 tablespoon brandy and the cream. Whip until stiff. Refrigerate.
3 Add 1 tablespoon brandy and 3 tablespoons icing sugar to the coffee in the measuring jug, then make it up to 120 ml/4 fl oz with water.
4 Lay 8 sponge fingers side by side on a plate, sprinkle liberally with coffee from the measuring jug and spread with ⅓ of the coffee cream.
5 Arrange 2 rows of sponge fingers (4 to each row) at right angles to, and on top of, the bottom layer. Sprinkle with coffee and spread with another ⅓ of the cream.
6 Arrange a final layer of the fingers side by side on top of the cream. Sprinkle with the remaining coffee and cover with the rest of the cream. Cover the dish with cling film and chill overnight.
7 Trim the edges of the cake neatly and decorate the top with more whipped cream and toasted almonds.
Serves 6

Drop In for a Drink

Nibbles and snacks to serve with drinks or cocktails.

HOT CHEESE TREATS

75 g/3 oz full fat soft cheese
1 egg yolk
2 tablespoons fresh double cream
1 level tablespoon grated or very finely
   chopped onion
2 level teaspoons flour
1 level teaspoon tomato purée
50 g/2 oz English Cheddar cheese, grated
salt and pepper
24 mini toasts, or 6 crisp biscuits or cream
   crackers cut into quarters
25 g/1 oz crisps, finely crushed
paprika

1 Preheat the oven to 200°C/400°F/Gas 6,
shelf above centre.
2 Combine the soft cheese with the egg yolk,
cream, onion and flour. Stir in the tomato
purée, ¾ of the cheese, then season to taste.
3 Divide the mixture between 24 mini
biscuits. Sprinkle the tops with the crisps,
remaining cheese and a dusting of paprika.
4 Bake the biscuits for about 10 minutes
until golden. Serve hot.
Makes 24

SHONA'S OLIVE PÂTÉ

This makes a delicious piquant spread which
will be consumed with gusto even by
non-olive lovers!

50 g/2 oz onion, chopped
125 g/4 oz English butter
175 g/6 oz pimiento-stuffed green olives
75 g/3 oz full fat soft cheese
3 tablespoons fresh double cream
salt and pepper

1 Gently fry the onion in the butter until soft,
but not coloured.
2 Tip the fried onion with the butter, olives,
cheese and cream into a food processor or
liquidiser and process until smoothly
blended. Season to taste with salt and
pepper.
3 Spoon the mixture into a dish, fork level,
then cover and chill until firm. Serve as a pâté
with hot toast or piled on to little biscuits to
eat with drinks.
Serves 6
Note: Instead of using a processor the
ingredients can all be finely chopped and
then mashed together before chilling.
   For another version, which I call *Pâté
Piccante*, use only 50 g/2 oz of the olives but
add 25 g/1 oz anchovy fillets, 2 tablespoons
capers and the finely grated rind of ½ lemon.
Make in the same way.

STILTON STUFFED MUSHROOMS

25 g/1 oz English butter, at room temperature
50 g/2 oz Blue Stilton cheese
4 teaspoons fresh double cream
salt and pepper
24 button mushrooms, stalks removed
paprika

1   Beat the butter until creamy, mash in the cheese and cream. Mix together until soft enough to spread.
2   Season the creamed cheese to taste, then pipe or use a teaspoon to pile a little into each mushroom cup. Dust with paprika.
Makes 24
Note: This creamed Blue Stilton cheese paste is also good sandwiched between seeded black grape halves or filled into mini strips of celery.

PEPPER AND LIVER SAUSAGE RINGS

170 g/6 oz green pepper (as evenly long and
   thin as possible)
125 g/4 oz liver sausage
75 g/3 oz full fat soft cheese
25 g/1 oz English butter, melted
½ level teaspoon curry powder
1 teaspoon Worcestershire sauce
50 g/2 oz breadcrumbs
1 teaspoon vinegar
1-2 tablespoons fresh single or double cream
salt and pepper
paprika

1   Cut a thin slice off either end and remove core and seeds from green pepper to leave a tube.
2   Mash the liver sausage with the cheese, mix in the melted butter, curry powder, Worcestershire sauce, breadcrumbs, vinegar and cream. When smoothly blended, season to taste with salt and pepper.
3   Spoon the mixture into the green pepper tube, packing it as firmly as possible. Wrap in cling film and refrigerate until firm.
4   Cut the stuffed green pepper into fairly thin slices and arrange on a plate to serve. Halve the slices if they are large. Dust each slice with paprika.
Makes about 15 slices

SALAMI CORNETS

65 g/2½ fl oz fresh double cream
75 g/3 oz full fat soft cheese
1 tablespoon thick mayonnaise
salt and pepper
16 very thin slices of salami
green or black olives to garnish (optional)

1   Whip the cream until stiff.
2   Mash the cheese smoothly with the mayonnaise. Fold in the cream and season well to taste with salt and pepper.
3   Carefully remove the skin from the salami and roll each slice into a cone shape.
4   Pipe or spoon the cheese cream into each cone and garnish with whole or chopped olives, if liked.
Makes 16

Stirred not Shaken

Amuse your friends with these sophisticated cream drinks ... which are not as innocent as they look!

CZAR'S DELIGHT

1 tablespoon vodka
1 tablespoon mint liqueur
75 ml/2½ fl oz fresh single cream
150 ml/¼ pint milk, chilled
crushed ice
frosted mint leaves

1 Mix together vodka, mint liqueur, cream and milk.
2 Place crushed ice in 2 glasses, pour over the cocktail. Decorate each glass with frosted mint leaves.
Serves 2

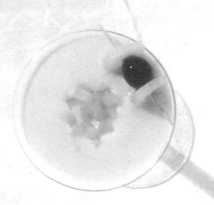

HAWAIIAN DREAM

300 ml/½ pint chilled milk
4 canned apricot halves, chopped
227-g/8-oz can pineapple chunks, drained
2 teaspoons lemon juice
2 tablespoons canned apricot syrup
3 tablespoons kirsch
2 tablespoons fresh single cream
crushed ice
maraschino cherries

1 Place milk, apricots, pineapple (leaving 4 pieces for garnish), lemon juice, apricot syrup, kirsch and cream in a blender.
2 Liquidise until smooth. Place crushed ice in 2 glasses and pour over the liquid. Garnish with remaining pineapple and cherries.
Serves 2

TEQUILA SPARKLE

1 beaten egg white
granulated sugar
2 tablespoons tequila
3 tablespoons coffee liqueur
150 ml/¼ pint fresh double cream
150 ml/¼ pint milk, chilled

DARK CARIBBEAN

2 tablespoons cocoa powder
1 tablespoon brown sugar
2 tablespoons dark rum
450 ml/¾ pint milk, chilled
2 tablespoons fresh single cream
2 slices lime
2 maraschino cherries

1 Mix together cocoa powder and sugar.
Add the rum.
2 Whisk in the milk and cream until frothy.
3 Pour into 2 glasses. Decorate each with a
slice of lime and a maraschino cherry.
Serves 2

STRAWBERRY PARADISE

4 tablespoons rum coconut liqueur
100 g/4 oz strawberries, fresh or canned
150 ml/¼ pint milk, chilled
150 ml/¼ pint fresh single cream
crushed ice

1 Place rum coconut liqueur, strawberries
(keeping 2 for decoration), milk and cream in
a blender. Liquidise until smooth.
2 Place crushed ice in 2 glasses. Pour over
the strawberry liquid. Serve each glass
garnished with a strawberry.
Serves 2

SPECIAL CREAM
CHOCOLATE

50 g/2 oz plain chocolate
½ teaspoon ground cinnamon
300 ml/½ pint milk
150 ml/5 fl oz fresh whipping cream
2 tablespoons brandy

1 Place the chocolate, half the cinnamon
and the milk in a saucepan. Heat gently until
the chocolate dissolves.
2 Bring to the boil.
3 Whip the cream until softly stiff and then
whisk most of it into the liquid.
4 Add the brandy. Pour into 2 glasses and
top with remaining cream and cinnamon.
Serves 2

1 Frost the tops of 2 glasses by dipping the
rims in a shallow dish of beaten egg white
and then into a dish of granulated sugar.
Allow the egg white to harden.
2 Mix together the tequila, coffee liqueur,
cream and milk.
3 Pour into the frosted glasses.
Serves 2

Central Heating

Warming dishes for cold weather.

TOASTED KIPPER CREAMS

450 g/1 lb kippers
25 g/1 oz English butter
25 g/1 oz flour
225 g/8 oz tomatoes, peeled and chopped
65 ml/2½ fl oz fresh single cream
salt and pepper
25-50 g/1-2 oz English Cheddar cheese,
    grated
cayenne pepper
toast (optional)

1 Place the kippers in a saucepan with
275 ml/½ pint water. Simmer for 5-10
minutes until the fish is cooked. Strain,
reserving stock.
2 Remove skin and bones from the fish.
Flake the flesh.
3 Cook the fish stock over a fairly high heat
to reduce to 150 ml/¼ pint.
4 Melt the butter, blend in the flour then the
reduced fish stock. Stir the sauce over a low
heat to make a very thick smooth sauce.
5 Stir the tomatoes, flaked kipper and all but
1 tablespoon of the cream into the sauce.
Season to taste with salt and pepper.
6 Divide the kipper mixture between 4-6
individual flameproof dishes. Dust the top of
each with grated cheese, a swirl of cream and
a dusting of cayenne pepper.
7 Just before serving grill the kipper creams
under a preheated grill until golden brown.
Serve hot with fingers of toast, if liked.
Serves 4-6

Note: Served with boiled rice and a green
salad the kipper cream makes a good main
dish for 4. To eliminate the fiddly boning
process, 225 g/8 oz kipper fillets can be used
instead of the whole fish – but they lack the
depth of flavour that makes this dish so good.

KIDNEYS IN A NIGHTSHIRT WITH MUSTARD SAUCE

6 lamb's kidneys, skinned
6 rashers streaky bacon, rinded
25 g/1 oz English butter
25 g/1 oz mushrooms, chopped
2 level teaspoons cornflour
150 ml/¼ pint stock
150 ml/5 fl oz fresh single cream
1 level tablespoon Dijon mustard
salt and pepper
215-g/7½-oz packet frozen puff pastry,
    thawed
beaten egg or milk to brush

1 Cut the kidneys almost in half and, using a
pair of scissors, cut away the cores.
2 Wrap each kidney firmly in a rasher of
streaky bacon and secure with a wooden
cocktail stick.
3 Gently heat the butter in a frying pan.
Place the kidneys in the pan with the loose
end of bacon down. Fry over a medium heat
to brown the bacon lightly on both sides.
4 Place the kidneys aside to cool then
remove the sticks.
5 To make the mustard sauce: fry the
chopped mushrooms in the pan the kidneys
were cooked in. Blend in the cornflour then
the stock. Bring the sauce to the boil, stirring.
Cool slightly then add the cream, mustard,
salt and pepper to taste. Place the sauce
aside.
6 Preheat the oven to 230°C/450°F/Gas 8,
shelf above centre.
7 Divide the pastry into 6 equal pieces and
roll each roughly to the size of a saucer. Place
the kidneys on one half of the pastry rounds
then fold over and seal the pastry together
with a little water. Place on a baking sheet.
8 Brush the parcels with beaten egg or milk
then bake for about 15 minutes until puffed
and golden.
9 Gently reheat the sauce without allowing
it to boil and serve it with the kidney and
bacon parcels. Broccoli and a creamed root
vegetable like parsnip or swede go well with
this dish.
Serves 6

HOT GOLDEN FRUIT SALAD WITH CINNAMON CREAM

450-g/16-oz can apricot halves
450-g/16-oz can Victoria plums
450-g/16-oz can mango or peaches, sliced
50 g/2 oz demerara sugar
1 orange
½ stick cinnamon
Cinnamon cream
150 ml/5 fl oz fresh double cream
2 tablespoons milk
1 tablespoon brandy
¼ level teaspoon ground cinnamon
2 level tablespoons brown sugar

1 Drain the can of apricots and plums together and reserve 425 ml/¾ pint of their juice. Drain the mango or peaches and add them to the fruit.
2 Gently heat the demerara sugar with 150 ml/¼ pint water, add the finely grated rind from ½ the orange and the stick of cinnamon. When the brown sugar has dissolved add the reserved syrup from the apricots and plums. Bring the syrup slowly to the boil.
3 Peel and thinly slice the orange then add it with the other fruit to the hot syrup. Heat gently until piping hot.
4 Meanwhile make the cinnamon cream: whip the cream with the milk until softly stiff, stir in the brandy, cinnamon and brown sugar. When softly stiff, place aside to serve with the hot fruit salad.
Serves 6-8
Note: A quick salad to make from the store cupboard. The secret of its success lies in the fact that you replace some of the rather rich canned juice with your own lighter syrup. You can use the juice to make a drink by whisking it into your favourite yogurt and topping it with whipped cream.

Supper Party on Ice

With these dishes in the freezer you are always in the position to ask friends to stay on for a meal — simply take out the dishes and heat them to serve without a thawing-out period.

CREAM OF SPINACH SOUP

275 ml/½ pint milk
50 g/2 oz onion, chopped
3 cloves
1 blade of mace
3 peppercorns
250-g/8.82-oz packet frozen (chopped or puréed) spinach or 350 g/12 oz fresh spinach
2 chicken stock cubes
25 g/1 oz English butter
25 g/1 oz flour
salt and pepper
grated nutmeg
65 ml/2½ fl oz fresh single cream

1 Very gently heat the milk for 10 minutes together with the onion, cloves, mace and peppercorns. Leave until cold then strain.
2 If using fresh spinach, cook it until barely tender then drain well and chop very finely.
3 Cook the fresh or frozen spinach in 575 ml/1 pint water with the stock cubes for about 5-10 minutes or until it is very tender. Place aside.
4 Melt the butter in a large saucepan over a medium heat. Remove the pan from the heat to smoothly blend in the flour, the strained milk and finally the spinach with the stock.
5 Stirring continuously, bring the soup to the boil then simmer gently for 5 minutes. Cool slightly then season to taste with salt, pepper and grated nutmeg. Stir in all but 2 tablespoons of the cream.
6 Ladle the soup into bowls and swirl a little cream in each to serve.
Serves 4-6
Note: To freeze: pour the soup into a plastic container, allowing about 2.5 cm/1 inch headroom. Cover and freeze until required. To serve: dip the plastic container in hot water to release the soup. Turn the solid block into a saucepan containing about 4 tablespoons cold water and heat very gently, stirring from time to time, until piping hot. In addition to serving this soup as a first course, it makes a complete light meal if you slice in some boiling sausage.

STRESA PORK

6 small slices of pork tenderloin
flour to coat
salt and pepper
about 100 g/4 oz English butter
225 g/8 oz mushrooms, thinly sliced
225 g/8 oz onions, finely chopped
125 g/4 oz streaky bacon, derinded and
    shredded
about 65 g/2½ oz flour
2-3 tablespoons dry sherry or stock
5 tablespoons stock
2 level tablespoons tomato purée
350 ml/12 fl oz milk
125 g/4 oz mature English Cheddar cheese,
    grated
150 ml/5 fl oz fresh single cream
watercress to garnish

1   Place the pork slices between sheets of
cling film and flatten as thinly as possible
with a meat bat or rolling pin. Coat them in
flour, seasoned with a little salt and pepper.
2   Melt about 25 g/1 oz of the butter in a large
frying pan and fry the meat slices quickly until
cooked through and browned on both sides.
Place in a shallow ovenproof dish.
3   Add more butter to the pan and fry the
sliced mushrooms over a high heat until they
are soft, then remove them from the pan with
a slotted spoon and place aside.

4   Fry the chopped onion until soft, add the
shredded bacon and continue to cook until
the onions are turning golden brown.
Remove the pan from the heat to stir in 1
level tablespoon of the flour, the sherry (or
stock) plus 5 further tablespoons of stock and
the tomato purée.
5   Continue cooking for 2-3 minutes until the
mixture is a thick paste. Season it well to
taste before spooning a little on top of each
slice. Top each with a layer of mushrooms.
Place the dish aside.
6   Preheat the oven to 200°C/400°F/Gas 6,
upper centre shelf.
7   Melt the remaining 50 g/2 oz butter over a
low heat, mix in the remaining 50 g/2 oz flour
and cook for 1 minute before removing the
pan from the heat to blend in the milk.
8   Return the pan to the heat and stir the
sauce continuously over a low heat until it
comes to the boil and thickens then stir in all
but 1 tablespoon of the grated cheese until it
melts. Cool slightly then stir in the cream.
9   Season the sauce to taste with salt and
pepper then place aside to cool further
before spooning it over each piece of meat.
Scatter the remaining cheese evenly over the
top of the meat.
10   Bake the pork for 20-30 minutes until the
cheese is lightly brown. Serve garnished with
watercress.
Serves 6

Note: To freeze: use a serving dish that will
withstand going from the freezer to the oven.
Cool the dish completely after stage 9; wrap
in foil and overwrap in a sealed polythene
bag. Freeze and store for up to 2 months.
To use: remove the polythene bag, loosen
the foil. Heat the dish in a preheated oven
200°C/400°F/Gas 6 for about 50 minutes.
Remove foil, increase heat to
230°C/450°F/Gas 8 then cook until the cheese
topping is bubbly and a bright golden-brown
colour.
Slices of veal fillet can be used instead of
pork tenderloin.

ANNE'S PAVLOVAS

4 egg whites (size 1, 2)
¼ level teaspoon salt
225 g/8 oz caster sugar
½ teaspoon vanilla essence
½ teaspoon vinegar
4 teaspoons cold water
275 ml/10 fl oz fresh double cream
65 ml/2½ fl oz fresh single cream
4-6 kiwi fruit, peeled and sliced
50 g/2 oz walnuts, chopped

1 Preheat the oven to 140°C/275°F/Gas 1, lowest shelves. Line 2 baking sheets with non-stick kitchen paper, or butter and dust with caster sugar.
2 Whisk the egg whites and salt together until *very* stiff.
3 Continue whisking steadily, adding the sugar a spoonful at a time and whisking well after each addition.
4 When all the sugar has been added, whisk in the vanilla essence, the vinegar and cold water.
5 Pile the mixture on to the baking sheet in 12 mounds about 7.5 cm/3 inches in diameter and 4 cm/1½ inches high. Shape them neatly with a spoon, pulling the sides out into spikes, if liked.
6 Cook the Pavlovas for about 1¼ hours until they feel crisp and firm. Leave in the oven until cold.
7 Carefully remove the Pavlovas from the paper and arrange them on a serving tray. Whip the creams together until softly stiff then pile each Pavlova high with the cream, sliced kiwi fruit and a sprinkling of chopped walnuts.
Serves 12

Note: These Pavlovas will have a crisp crust with a marshmallowy centre. My New Zealand friend, who originally gave me the recipe, cooks hers for just 5 minutes in the centre of a preheated oven 180°C/350°F/Gas 4 and then leaves them in the closed oven (without opening the door) for 1 hour. Cooked this way the Pavlovas are marshmallowy all the way through.

BRANDIED BOMBE VESUVIUS

A spectacular dish to be served with lights out!

284 ml/10 fl oz fresh double cream
25 g/1 oz icing sugar, sifted
4 egg whites
2 tablespoons brandy (or 1 teaspoon vanilla essence or 150 ml/¼ pint sweetened strawberry purée)
1 bought sponge flan case
3 tablespoons jam
125 g/4 oz caster sugar
2 tablespoons brandy (to flame)

1 Place the well chilled cream in a bowl, add the icing sugar and whip until stiff. Cover and refrigerate.

2 Whisk 2 of the egg whites until very stiff and meringue-like then fold in the whipped cream and brandy or vanilla essence or strawberry purée.

3 Turn the fluffy cream mixture into a 1.1 litre/2 pint pudding basin and freeze until solid.

4 Rest the sponge flan case on the loose base of a flan tin, trim round the inside, if necessary, so it will accommodate the iced cream neatly. Spread thickly with the jam.

5 Dip the basin of iced cream quickly in hot water, run a knife round the inside of the basin and turn the frozen cream on top of the flan. Freeze.

6 Whisk the remaining 2 egg whites until very stiff, add 90 g/3½ oz of the caster sugar very gradually, about a tablespoon at a time, whisking well after each addition.

7 Either pipe or spread this meringue thickly over the iced cream and sides of the flan to cover completely.

8 Return the bombe to the freezer. When frozen, cover with an upturned plastic box or make a bonnet of foil to protect the meringue for storage period.

9 About 1 hour before the bombe is required for serving, preheat the oven to 220°C/425°F/Gas 7 and cook it for 5 minutes or until meringue is evenly browned. The bombe is now safe to leave for up to 45 minutes without melting.

10 Before serving, pour the remaining 2 tablespoons of brandy in a jug and stand this in a pan of hot water. Sprinkle the remaining caster sugar and then the hot brandy, over the meringue. Set light to it and serve immediately.

Serves 6

Something to Celebrate?

*A special celebration menu
to serve* 12.

TOMATO, AVOCADO AND CRAB SOUP

2 large ripe avocados
850 ml/1 ½ pints well flavoured chicken stock
    (or use water and 2 stock cubes)
3-4 tablespoons lemon juice
900 g/2 lb tomatoes
25 g/1 oz onion, finely chopped or grated
125-g/4-oz packet frozen crab meat, thawed
2 tablespoons Worcestershire sauce
275 ml/10 fl oz fresh single cream
salt and pepper
chopped parsley to garnish

1   Peel the avocados, cut in half to remove the stone then mash smoothly. Gradually blend in the stock and lemon juice.
2   Dip the tomatoes in boiling water for a few seconds then peel, seed and finely chop them. Add to the soup with the onion.
3   Reserve half the *brown* crab meat then stir all the rest with the Worcestershire sauce and ¾ of the cream into the soup. Season well with salt and pepper. Cover and chill the soup.
4   Before serving mix the reserved brown crab meat with the remaining cream, swirl into the soup and sprinkle with parsley.
Serves 12

Note: Terribly simple and terribly good! The only snag is it does discolour a little if made much in advance. However, if the soup is made not more than 4 hours before required and left covered with the avocado stone in it, it will be quite all right. Remove the stone before serving.

LES PETITS POULETS D'ARGENT (Little Silver Chickens)

This dish is good served with asparagus or mangetout peas and new potatoes.

12 boned chicken breasts
flour to coat
salt and pepper
125 g/4 oz English butter
150 ml/5 fl oz fresh double cream
2 fresh limes or 1 large lemon
1-2 large cloves garlic, crushed
2 tablespoons finely chopped parsley or
    3 level teaspoons dried parsley
2 teaspoons finely chopped fresh thyme
    or ½ level teaspoon dried thyme
4 tablespoons very finely chopped onion
12 sprigs of thyme
large roll of foil

1   Preheat the oven to 180°C/350°F/Gas 4, centre shelf.
2   Roll the chicken breasts in flour seasoned with salt and pepper.
3   Melt some of the butter in a frying pan and fry the chicken in batches, over a fairly high heat; add more butter as necessary, until they are brown on all sides.
4   Whip the cream until softly stiff, add the finely grated rind from the limes or lemon with 4 tablespoons of the juice, the crushed garlic, parsley, chopped or dried thyme and the onion. Season to taste with salt.
5   Cut 12 rectangular sheets of foil about 30 x 35 cm/12 x 14 inches.
6   Place the chicken breasts on the sheets of foil then spoon the cream mixture on each, topped with a slice of lime or lemon and a sprig of thyme. Now bring the foil up and over the chicken to make long sausages. Fold the top edges together. Twist one end of the foil into a chicken head shape and fan the other end into a tail, taking care not to tear the foil.
8   Arrange the parcels on a wire rack resting over a roasting tin containing about 2.5 cm/1 inch of water. Bake for about 40 minutes or until the chicken is tender.
Serves 12

LEMON SURPRISE

2 large juicy lemons
3 eggs, separated
125 g/4 oz caster sugar
284 ml/10 fl oz fresh double cream
150 ml/5 fl oz fresh single cream
Meringues
2 egg whites
125 g/4 oz caster sugar

1 Finely grate the rind and squeeze the juice from the lemons.

2 Whisk the egg whites until *very* stiff then add the caster sugar a spoonful at a time, whisking well after each addition, until the mixture is very thick.

3 Whisk both creams together until softly stiff. Place aside about ⅓ of this cream then combine the remaining ⅔ with the egg yolks and mix well together. Then fold it evenly and smoothly into the whisked whites with the lemon rind and juice.

4 Turn the mixture into a 1.1 litre/2 pint pudding basin, cover and freeze until firm.

5 To make the meringues: preheat the oven to 120°C/250°F/Gas ½, shelf below centre. Whisk the egg whites until very stiff then add the caster sugar gradually, whisking very well after each addition. Pipe or spoon blobs of the mixture (about the size of a 10p piece) on baking sheets lined with non-stick kitchen paper. Bake the meringues for about 2 hours or until they are dry and crisp. Remove the meringues from the baking tray carefully and leave them to cool on a wire tray.

6 Dip the pudding basin containing the lemon mixture quickly in and out of hot water, run a knife round the edge and turn the lemon cream out on to a serving plate (if the surface seems at all sticky, return the cream to the freezer for another 30 minutes or until it is firm again).

7 Spread the reserved cream over the surface of the lemon cream then cover with the meringues.

8 Leave the bombe for about 30 minutes before serving; this will mean that the centre will be soft enough to slice. If you like you can decorate the top of the bombe with a posy of fresh flowers.

Serves 8-12

Note: I made this dessert for my parents' Golden Wedding Anniversary and topped it with tiny golden garnet roses.

SWEDISH CHOCOLATE TORTE

50 g/2 oz blanched and flaked almonds
50 g/2 oz raisins
50 g/2 oz glacé cherries, chopped
2 packets boudoir biscuits, broken into
    quarters (36 fingers)
4 tablespoons brandy (optional)
2 tablespoons orange squash
100 g/3½ oz plain dessert chocolate
225 g/8 oz English butter, softened
4 egg yolks
125 g/4 oz caster sugar
3 level tablespoons cocoa powder
150 ml/5 fl oz fresh double cream
3 tablespoons milk

1 Toast the blanched almonds by spreading them on a sheet of foil and placing them under the grill. Keep a careful watch and turn frequently.

2 Place the raisins, half the toasted almonds, the glacé cherries and boudoir biscuits in a bowl. Spoon the brandy, if using, and orange squash over them. Turn with a spoon from time to time so that the liquid is absorbed.

3 Place the chocolate, broken into pieces, in a bowl. Stand the bowl over a pan of hot water making sure that the bowl is not actually touching the water. Heat very gently until the chocolate has melted.

4 Cream the butter until very soft then stir in the melted chocolate.

5 Whisk the egg yolks with the caster sugar until much paler, thick and foamy then carefully stir in the chocolate butter, the cocoa and the ingredients from the bowl.

6 Turn the mixture into a 1.1 litre/2 pint cake tin, smooth over the top, cover with cling film and refrigerate until firm.

7 Dip the tin in hot water for a few seconds, loosen round the cake with a knife then turn it out on to a plate and place in the refrigerator.

8 Whip the cream with the milk until softly stiff. Remove the cake from the refrigerator and spread the top with a layer of the whipped cream then pipe the remainder round the edge. Scatter the centre with the remaining toasted almonds. If it suits the occasion, decorate with candles.

Serves 8-12

Note: This is a very rich cake so only cut it into small portions. For a change try adding a little chopped candied peel or crystallised ginger. Microwave owners can melt the chocolate very easily by breaking it into a basin and placing it in the oven at Full for 2 minutes. Stir and use.

Help Yourself

A choice of reasonably priced buffet dishes that will satisfy a crowd of 25.

THAI CHICKEN

10-12 chicken quarters (leg portions)
350 g/12 oz onions, chopped
3 cloves garlic, crushed (optional)
¾ level tablespoon flour
75 g/3 oz crunchy peanut butter
396-g/14-oz can tomatoes
227-g/8-oz can tomatoes
1½ level teaspoons turmeric
1½ level teaspoons ground cumin
¾ level teaspoon ground cardamom
¾ level teaspoon chilli powder
½ level teaspoon black pepper
1½ level teaspoons brown sugar
3 tablespoons vinegar
4-5 tablespoons soy sauce
1½ chicken stock cubes
1 cucumber (about 450 g/1 lb)
275 ml/10 fl oz fresh single cream
4 teaspoons lemon juice
2 level teaspoons caster sugar
salt and pepper
canned sliced mango

Pilaff
350 g/12 oz onions, finely chopped
500 g/1 lb 2 oz long grain rice
75 g/3 oz English butter
2 chicken stock cubes
Sambals
sweet chutney
peanuts
sliced banana in lemon juice
sliced or chopped green pepper
grated coconut
prawn crisps

1 Preheat the oven to 180°C/350°F/Gas 4, shelf below centre.
2 Cut the chicken quarters in half into neat leg and thigh joints; arrange them in a large shallow heatproof dish.
3 Combine in a bowl the chopped onions, garlic, flour and peanut butter. Add both cans of tomatoes with their juice and smoothly blend together. Stir in the turmeric, cumin, cardamom, chilli, pepper, sugar, vinegar, soy sauce and stock cubes.
4 Pour this sauce over the chicken, cover with foil and place in the oven. Cook for about 1½ hours or until the chicken is very tender.
5 Make the pilaff about 45 minutes before the chicken is ready: place the chopped onions in a large casserole with the rice and butter. Cover and place in the oven for about

LAMB WITH WHEAT AND WALNUTS

350 g/12 oz bulgur cracked wheat
450 g/1 lb aubergine
salt and pepper
450 g/1 lb onions, sliced
900 g/2 lb boneless lamb, cut into small
   chunks
8 tablespoons oil
2 tablespoons vinegar
450-g/16-oz can tomatoes
125 g/4 oz raisins
125 g/4 oz walnuts
ground cinnamon
2-3 cloves garlic, crushed (optional)
150 ml/5 fl oz soured cream
lemon wedges
chopped fresh mint
cos lettuce to serve

15 minutes or until the onion is soft. Stir from time to time. Remove the casserole from the oven and stir in the chicken stock cubes and 1.25 litres/2¼ pints boiling water. Stir, cover the casserole and return to the oven for about 30 minutes or until the rice is cooked, with fluffy, separate grains, and the stock has been absorbed.

6 To make the cucumber sauce: coarsely grate the cucumber and leave to drain for at least 30 minutes. Tip all but about 4-5 tablespoons of the cream into a bowl. Stir in the lemon juice. Just before serving the sauce, stir the cucumber, sugar, salt and pepper into the cream.

7 Turn the pilaff on to a large hot serving dish. Lift the chicken portions from the sauce and arrange on top of the rice. Stir the reserved cream into the spicy tomato sauce, check the seasoning then spoon this over the chicken portions.

8 Serve the Thai chicken with the cucumber sauce and sliced mango, plus any or all of the sambal side dishes.
Serves 12-15 (Make double quantity for 25)

Note: Chicken in this unusual, hot, spicy sauce is a good dish to serve to friends who like something a little different.

   Do not be tempted to leave out the mango or cucumber salad as they give the finishing touch to the flavour balance.

1 Soak the cracked wheat in cold water for 30 minutes. Drain well.

2 Quarter and slice the unpeeled aubergine then place in a colander and sprinkle with 1 level teaspoon salt. Leave for 15 minutes, rinse in cold water then pat dry in a teatowel.

3 Fry the onion and lamb in some of the oil until cooked and brown then remove from the frying pan to a plate.

4 Fry the aubergine in the pan with more oil as necessary until it is soft, then remove it to the plate and sprinkle with the vinegar.

5 Place the canned tomatoes in the frying pan and add the drained wheat. Heat gently then stir in the raisins and walnuts. Season very well to taste with the cinnamon, salt, pepper and garlic, if used.

6 Pile the lamb and wheat mixture on to a hot serving plate, top with soured cream and lemon wedges sprinkled with the mint. Serve with a bowl of cos lettuce.
Serves 12 (Make double quantity for 25)

Note: In order to bring out the nutty flavour of the wheat, it is important to season this dish well, particularly with salt.

CHUNKY DUNK SALAD WITH THOUSAND ISLAND DIP

Thousand Island Dip:
150 ml/¼ pint mayonnaise
150 ml/5 fl oz fresh double or soured cream
1 tablespoon lemon juice
¼ level teaspoon paprika
2 rounded tablespoons tomato ketchup
6 pimiento-stuffed olives or 4 gherkins, very finely chopped
2 level teaspoons horseradish sauce
2 teaspoons finely chopped chives or 1 teaspoon very finely chopped onion
1 clove garlic, crushed
salt and pepper
Salad
575 g/1¼ lb tiny new potatoes
350 g/12 oz unpeeled prawns
4 hard-boiled eggs
6 sticks celery
6 young courgettes
4 carrots
1 small cucumber
1 head of chicory
1-2 avocados
2 tablespoons French dressing

1 To make the thousand island dip: combine the mayonnaise in a bowl with the cream, lemon juice, paprika, ketchup, olives, horseradish, chives, and garlic and season to taste with salt and pepper. Cover the bowl with cling film and refrigerate.
2 Scrub the new potatoes then boil in salted water until they are just tender. Drain and leave aside until cold.
3 Peel the prawns, leaving on the tails, halve the eggs, prepare and cut the celery, courgettes, carrots and cucumber into fingers. Separate the chicory leaves. Cover the salad ingredients with cling film until required.
4 Just before serving, peel and slice the avocado then dip it and the other salad ingredients in the French dressing.
5 Remove the cling film from the thousand island dip, stir well, spoon it into a serving bowl and place in the centre of a plate. Arrange the salad ingredients around this in groups.
Serves 12 (See Note)

Note: This quantity serves 12 but if it is used as a starter to be passed round with drinks, it will serve 25. To make it into a complete meal, stir 675 g/1½ lb cottage cheese and 450 g/1 lb canned tuna into the dip. Turn the mixture on to a bed of lettuce and garnish with prawns, lemon, tomato and hard-boiled egg. Serve the other ingredients as a salad.

SALMON MOUSSE

198-g/7-oz packet frozen cod steaks, thawed
5 tablespoons white wine or dry cider
1 bayleaf
salt and pepper
450-g/16-oz can salmon
milk
25 g/1 oz English butter
25 g/1 oz flour
3 level teaspoons (1 envelope) gelatine
3 rounded tablespoons thick mayonnaise
1 lemon
1 rounded tablespoon tomato purée
150 ml/5 fl oz fresh single cream
2 egg whites
parsley, tomato, cucumber and lemon to
    garnish

1 Place the fish steaks in a saucepan. Make the wine or cider up to 150 ml/¼ pint with cold water and pour it over the fish; add the bayleaf, salt and pepper. Bring very slowly to the boil then simmer gently for about 5 minutes or until the fish is cooked. Cool.
2 Drain the liquid both from the canned salmon and cooked fish into a measuring jug. Make it up to 275 ml/½ pint with milk as necessary.
3 Mash the salmon and cod finely with a fork, discarding skin and bones.

4 Melt the butter in a saucepan, remove from heat and stir in flour. Blend in the fish stock and milk mixture, a little at a time, to make a smooth sauce. Bring to boil, stirring, cook for 2 minutes. Cool, covered with damp greaseproof paper or cling film.
5 Soak the gelatine with 2 tablespoons water in a cup. Stand the cup in a pan of water, heat gently until dissolved.
6 Stir the mayonnaise, juice from ½ the lemon, the tomato purée, mashed fish, cream and gelatine into the sauce. Season to taste and place aside until just beginning to set.
7 Whisk the egg whites until softly stiff; fold them into the semi-set sauce mixture. Turn into an oiled 1.75 litre/3 pint soufflé dish or cake tin and leave aside in a cool place until set.
8 Dip the dish containing the mousse into hot water then run a knife around the inside and turn it upside down on to a serving plate. If the mousse does not drop out immediately, give a firm shake from side to side.
9 Garnish the mousse with sprigs of parsley and very thin slices of tomato, cucumber and zest of lemon.
Serves 12 (make double quantity for 25)

Note: This mousse also looks attractive made in a fish-shaped mould.

MEXICAN-STYLE BEEF WITH SIDE DISHES

6 tablespoons cooking oil
450 g/1 lb onions, sliced
225 g/8 oz streaky bacon, shredded
900 g/2 lb minced beef
3-4 cloves garlic, crushed
450-g/16-oz can baked beans
50 g/2 oz sultanas
2 bayleaves
4 level teaspoons demerara sugar
2 level teaspoons chilli powder
2 tablespoons tomato purée
575 ml/1 pint stock (or water and stock cube)
salt and pepper
675 g/1½ lb long grain rice
50 g/2 oz English butter
50 g/2 oz English Cheddar cheese, grated
275 ml/10 fl oz fresh double or soured cream
450-g/16-oz can tomatoes
2 green peppers
2-3 avocados
2 tablespoons lemon juice
1 small lettuce
three 396-g/14-oz cans red kidney beans
225 g/8 oz *very* finely chopped onion and chives mixed
paprika

1 Heat the oil in a very large, heavy saucepan and fry the onions gently until soft. Increase the heat and add the bacon. Continue frying until both bacon and onion are starting to brown. Remove to a plate with a slotted spoon.
2 Fry the minced beef over a high heat for about 4 minutes, turning it frequently.
3 Return the bacon and onion to the pan, stir in the garlic, baked beans, sultanas, bayleaves, sugar, chilli, tomato purée and stock. Cover the pan and simmer gently for 1 hour or until the meat is very tender. Season to taste with salt and pepper. Keep hot.
4 Bring a pan of salted water to the boil and boil the long grain rice for about 12 minutes or until just tender. Drain it well then stir in the butter, cheese, 2 tablespoons of the cream, salt and pepper to taste. Keep hot.
5 Meanwhile, prepare the side dishes and place each in a separate bowl: a – Whip the remaining double cream until softly stiff. b – Mash the canned tomatoes and their juice together. Season well with salt and pepper. c – Thinly slice the green pepper. d – Peel and slice the avocados, brush with lemon juice. e – Shred the lettuce finely. f – Heat then drain the kidney beans. g – Sprinkle the chopped onion with a little paprika.
6 Spoon the rice round the edge of a large, shallow hot serving dish and pour the chilli beef in the centre. Serve with all the separate side dishes.
Serves 12 (make double quantity for 25)
Note: Like a curry, this dish is not complete without all its side dishes. If you can get them, also include some Mexican Tostadas.

TESSA'S LEMON CRUNCH PIE

200 g/7 oz digestive biscuits, crumbled
175 g/6 oz demerara sugar
65 g/2½ oz English butter, melted
3 eggs, separated
275 ml/10 fl oz fresh double cream
finely grated rind and juice of 2 lemons
lemon slices to decorate

1 Place the crumbed digestive biscuits in a bowl with 50 g/2 oz of the sugar, add the butter. Stir and leave aside.
2 Whisk the egg yolks until thick and foamy. Add the remaining sugar gradually, whisking well after each addition.
3 Whip the cream until softly stiff then fold in the egg yolk mixture, the finely grated rind from both lemons and 6 tablespoons lemon juice.
4 Whisk the egg whites until very stiff, then fold them evenly into the lemon cream mixture.
5 Sprinkle a layer of the crumbs in the bottom of a 1.5 litre/3 pint serving bowl. Spread with a layer of the cream mixture then repeat alternate layers of crumb and cream until it is all used up. Cover and chill in the refrigerator for at least 4 hours before serving. Decorate with lemon slices.
Serves 12 (Make double quantity for 25)

Christmas Alternatives

It's hard to beat the traditional dishes of Christmas, but any one of these recipes retains the spirit of Christmas while making it just that bit different.

STUFFED TURKEY FILLETS WITH CHESTNUT SAUCE

125 g/4 oz pork sausagemeat
75 g/3 oz onion, finely chopped
¼ level teaspoon dried sage
15 g/½ oz fresh breadcrumbs
salt and pepper
flour
4 rashers streaky bacon
75 g/3 oz English butter
4 turkey fillets
50 g/2 oz button mushrooms, thinly sliced
125 g/4 oz cooked chestnuts, peeled and
   chopped
1 level tablespoon flour
1 tablespoon brandy
150 ml/¼ pint chicken stock
65 ml/2½ fl oz fresh single cream

1 Mash the sausagemeat with 25 g/1 oz of the onion, the sage and crumbs then season with salt and pepper. Divide the mixture equally into 4 and roll into fingers on a floured board. Wrap each 'finger' in a rasher of streaky bacon.
2 Melt 50 g/2 oz of the butter and fry the fingers on all sides until the bacon is golden.
3 Slit the turkey fillets almost in half horizontally and sandwich a 'finger' in each. Hold together with a wooden cocktail stick.
4 Roll the stuffed fillets in flour then fry slowly until cooked through and browned on all sides. Remove from pan and keep them hot in a hot serving dish. Remove the sticks.

5 Add more butter to the pan, if necessary, and gently fry the remaining onion, the mushrooms and chestnuts. When tender, stir in the tablespoon of flour then blend in the brandy, stock and cream. Bubble up, stirring until thick. Season the sauce to taste and pour over the turkey to serve.

Serves 4

Note: This dish can be prepared in advance. Refrigerate the turkey and sauce separately. Reheat the covered turkey in the oven, while the sauce is gently being heated on the hob.

SEAFOOD SALAD IN SOURED CREAM DRESSING

1 tablespoon oil
1 teaspoon lemon juice or vinegar
pepper and salt
1 level teaspoon very finely chopped capers
1 red dessert apple, cored and diced
15 g/½ oz onion, very finely chopped
125 g/4 oz shelled prawns
5 cm/2 inches cucumber, diced
1 stick celery chopped
2 hard-boiled eggs
150 ml/5 fl oz soured cream
½ teaspoon anchovy essence (optional)
lettuce leaves
paprika

1 Combine the oil and lemon juice or vinegar in a bowl, add plenty of freshly ground black pepper and salt then the finely chopped capers.

2 Add the apple, onion, prawns, cucumber and celery to the bowl. Turn together.

3 Thinly slice the hard-boiled eggs and, reserving 6 of the best slices, add the remainder to the salad with the soured cream and anchovy essence, if using. Stir together then cover with cling film and chill until required.

4 Arrange some freshly washed and torn lettuce leaves in 6 individual dishes or scallop shells, top with some of the salad then garnish each with reserved sliced egg and a shake of paprika.

Serves 6

Note: This salad is equally good made with canned tuna fish or salmon

CREAMED STILTON MOUSSE

15 g/½ oz (1 envelope) gelatine
1 chicken stock cube
225 g/8 oz Blue Stilton cheese
150 ml/5 fl oz fresh double cream
1 egg white
watercress

1 Brush a 1 litre/¾ pint ring mould with oil.
2 Place the gelatine in a measuring jug, stir in 3 tablespoons cold water, leave aside for 5 minutes to swell then bring up to 275 ml/½ pint with boiling water. Add the stock cube and stir until both gelatine and stock cube have dissolved. Leave aside until cold.
3 Mash the cheese well then, little by little, mix the cold gelatine mixture into it until smoothly blended. Refrigerate until *just* starting to set.
4 Whip the cream until softly stiff and fold it into the cheese mixture.
5 Whisk the egg white until very stiff and meringue-like then fold it into the cheese mixture.
6 Turn the cheese mousse into the prepared ring mould. Cover and refrigerate until firmly set.
7 Turn the mousse out on to a serving dish and fill the centre with watercress. Serve with crisp savoury biscuits, wholewheat Melba toast or granary bread.
Serves 4-6

CHESTNUT ROULADE CHANTILLY

225-g/8-oz can chestnut purée (sweetened)
3 eggs, separated
50 g/2 oz caster sugar
1 level teaspoon gelatine
1 level tablespoon icing sugar, sifted
150 ml/5 fl oz fresh double cream
150 ml/5 fl oz fresh whipping cream
sifted icing sugar to dust

1 Preheat the oven to 180°C/350°F/Gas 4, shelf above centre. Grease and line a Swiss

roll tin 23 x 33 cm/9 x 13 inches with non-stick kitchen paper. The paper should be cut to give a depth of 4 cm/1½ inches.
2 Mash the chestnut purée to soften, then beat until smooth with the egg yolks and caster sugar.
3 Whisk the egg whites until *very* stiff then fold them evenly into the chestnut mixture.
4 Lightly spread the mixture in the prepared tin. Bake for about 20 minutes or until well risen, golden and firm to a light touch.
5 Cover the hot cake with cling film and leave overnight.
6 Stir the gelatine in a basin with 2 teaspoons cold water, leave to swell. Stir in 1 tablespoon boiling water to dissolve the gelatine; stir in the icing sugar.
7 When the gelatine mixture is cool, add both the creams and whip until thick.
8 Turn the roulade out on to a worktop, carefully remove the paper then neatly trim round the edges with a sharp knife. Spread the roulade with the whipped cream and carefully roll it up. Dust heavily with icing sugar to serve.
Serves 6

Note: This roulade freezes well so can be made up to a month in advance of Christmas.

TURNABOUT CHOCOLATE TRIFLE

1 chocolate Swiss roll
2 tablespoons brandy
1 orange jelly (to make 575 ml/1 pint)
312-g/11-oz can mandarins
finely grated rind and juice of 1 large orange
1 egg, separated
1½ level tablespoons custard powder
2 level tablespoons sugar
275 ml/½ pint milk
50 g/2 oz ratafias or macaroons, crumbled
150 ml/5 fl oz fresh double cream
2 tablespoons sherry
1 level tablespoon icing sugar, sifted
drinking chocolate powder (optional)

1 Slice the Swiss roll, sprinkle with the brandy. Cover and place aside.
2 Break the jelly into pieces in a saucepan, add 150 ml/¼ pint water and stir over a gentle heat until melted. Stir in the juice from the mandarins, the finely grated rind and orange juice. Make the jelly up to 575 ml/1 pint with water then refrigerate until syrupy and starting to set.
3 Blend the egg yolk smoothly with the custard powder, sugar and 2 tablespoons of the milk. Heat the remaining milk until almost boiling then stir into the blended mixture. Return the custard to a gentle heat and stir until thick. Place aside to cool.
4 Pour ⅓ of the setting jelly into a 1.4 litre/ 2½ pint pudding basin. Spoon ⅓ of the Swiss roll into the jelly, cover with ⅓ of the drained mandarins, custard and crumbled ratafias. Spoon another ⅓ of jelly into the basin and layer in the remaining ⅔ Swiss roll, mandarins, custard and ratafias. Top with the remaining jelly.
5 Cover the basin and refrigerate overnight until firmly set.
6 Whisk the egg white very stiffly. Whip the cream until stiff with the sherry and icing sugar then fold in the egg white.
7 Coat the trifle with the cream mixture, swirling it attractively. Decorate the top with a sprig of holly if to be served as a Christmas trifle or dust with drinking chocolate.
Serves 8-10

Index

Acknowledgements

Photography by Charlie Stebbings
Photographic stylist Liz Allen-Eslor
Food prepared by Caroline Ellwood
'Children's Party Cakes' and 'Cream
Teas' cakes prepared by Lorna Walker.

The publishers would also like to express their gratitude to the
following for the loan of accessories for photography: The Craftsmen
Potters Association of Great Britain; The Reject Shop, London, SW3;
Putnams Kitchen Antiques, London, NW6; The Cocktail Shop,
London, W1; Harvey Nichols Ltd., London, SW1; Elizabeth David
Ltd., London, SW1; Covent Garden Kitchen Supplies, London, WC2;
Graham and Green, London, W11; Sloane Square Tiles, London,
SW3; Divertimenti, London, W1; World's End Tiles, London, SW8.